YOU DON'T HAVE TO DIE POOR

Powerful Strategies Toward
Financial Freedom & Prosperity

Rico D. Beans

The information offered in this book regarding financial and investment advice is solely the opinions of the author. The information does not constitute legal or financial advice and should not be used without first consulting with a financial professional to determine what may be best for your individual needs.

This book is dedicated to the following people:

My mother and aunt, who always encouraged me to learn and be the best at any endeavor. Your memory and legacy will forever live on in your children. We know that you are smiling down on us. My family for believing in my dreams.

Table of Contents

Introduction
From Poverty to Prosperity

I grew up in poverty, and I didn't always know it. It only became apparent to me when I was about seven or eight years old. I watched tears pouring down my mother's face like rain water on a brick wall during her attempt to remain calm. Being concerned, I asked my mother what was wrong, but she simply replied, "Everything will be fine," as she swallowed deeply, trying to keep the anger and frustration inside of her from exploding like a nuclear bomb. My mother, a single parent of four children, had lost her job working hourly at the local Sanyo manufacturing facility, which forced us to move out of our cozy little house into a housing project, living off government assistance.

It was a tough time for my siblings and me. Money was scarce, and often I was not allowed to go for a second helping of dinner, even though I was still hungry. Sometimes I noticed my mother did not eat, although she told us she wasn't hungry. We lived in an area where the average income was below the poverty line, without many options for employment.

A few years after moving to the housing projects, I witnessed my mother pass away from a stroke at the age of 39. She died financially poor. I would eventually move in with my aunt, her husband, and three cousins following my mother's untimely death. I was uncertain of how my life will unfold after my mom's death.

Nevertheless, I thought that living with my aunt meant things would be different. Unfortunately, I was somewhat mistaken in that assumption. I was grateful to my aunt for allowing me to live with her family, but things were tight financially at my aunt's house. She was going to school to get her degree in education and my uncle, a self-employed plumber, was the only one working to support the household.

Early one morning, I woke up and excitedly got dressed for school. I ironed my jeans with starch until they were hard enough to stand on their own like a cardboard cutout. I had just finished brushing my hair when my aunt yelled that it was time to catch the school bus. My cousins and I stood at the door, waiting for my aunt to give us our lunch money. Unfortunately, she only had enough to provide us with three dollars and fifty cents. I remember thinking, "Three dollars and fifty cents. That is all she gave us!" I looked in disbelief as my aunt handed my cousins and me the money to cover our meals for the week, which was nowhere near enough.

One thing about growing up poor is that it teaches you to become resourceful. Instead of complaining about it, my philosophy was that there was a solution to every problem. Every Monday, I would not eat lunch; instead, I would take my lunch money to one of the neighborhood convenience stores with very low prices to buy snacks and sell them at school for a higher price. During that time, one of my favorite actors was Eddie Murphy. In the movie, *Trading Places*, starring Eddie Murphy, the character Winthorpe, played by Dan Aykroyd, said, "Buy low, sell high." So that's exactly what I did! I became a budding entrepreneur and a hustler—learning how to maximize the money I earned and multiply it.

I would also learn to make money doing various jobs around the neighborhood, like cutting grass, that I could use to invest in my business. Working often meant I could not play neighborhood sports or video games as often as other kids. This experience sparked my curiosity regarding money and economics. I vowed then never to live in poverty when I became an adult. I learned the art of entrepreneurship; it coursed through my blood.

By the time I reached my early twenties, I had begun to invest in financial education from finance books, experience, and learning from others. Coming from a military family, I would eventually join the United States Air Force, commissioning as a 2nd Lieutenant during the height of Operation Enduring Freedom. I was immediately assigned to the brave men and women of the 5th Combat Communications. During a deployment to Afghanistan, I would meet a senior noncommissioned officer who would spark my interest in investing in the financial markets. He would often say, “LT, you need to invest in the market. I am making money while I sleep. If you start now, by the time you retire, you will be in good shape financially.” He taught me that making money wasn’t enough but that you needed to make your money work for you by letting your money produce even more money for you without you touching it. So, I started investing in mutual funds, stocks, and bonds—by the time I was 24, I had built up a healthy portfolio. That same year, my aunt, who raised me, died from cancer. Similar to my mother, she also died poor.

Once I turned 25 years old, I moved into purchasing real estate and bought my first investment property in South Carolina. Eventually, I would learn to start simple cash flow businesses to create multiple income streams.

I remember coming home after four months of being deployed to Afghanistan in a war zone. The following Sunday, I went to church, where I heard an inspiring message telling me to dream “God-size dreams” and that I was destined for more.

These words planted a seed that would forever change my life. At that very moment, I realized I didn’t want prosperity to be a mere dream. I wanted it to be a reality! It would take a shift in mindset, financial literacy, and a lot of hard work, but I was going to create a different path for myself and the generations to follow.

My goals are to create assets my family can benefit from long after I am no longer living. And I want to help you do the same, too, because I know you love your family just as much as I love mine. Prosperity shouldn’t just be nice words—it should be a reality.

This book is for anyone who doesn't want to work an entire lifetime only to die poor. You have decided you are willing to shift your mindset and increase your financial literacy to achieve prosperity. You are someone who grew up seeing a lot of poverty like me, or perhaps you are doing well but want to make improvements that lead to more financial freedom and a better life for your children.

Let Me Help You Turn Prosperity from Words To Action

In this book, I will share a philosophy that will shift your current mindset to a *wealth* mindset—prosperity begins with the mind first. Once you understand the thought process required for prosperity and wealth, I will teach you to take control and manage your finances like a CEO. I give you tips and tools to make better decisions on managing your money and some tested philosophies on budgeting, managing debt, saving, and investing. I have also included some metrics and rules of thumb that have proven valuable for investment practitioners and high-net-worth people (HNWI).

While budgeting and managing the money you earn is foundational to wealth creation, the biggest and often overlooked challenge to long-term wealth creation is that many people lack income, even after proper budgeting. Subsequently, they don't acquire the assets that lead to generational wealth. Therefore, I give you practical tips to create new income streams to increase your ability to invest in assets. I also teach you about the various sources of income, the pros and cons of each source, and how to obtain them.

Since business ownership is paramount, I provide step-by-step guidance on the basics of creating a business and some simple business types that you can start without having a lot of capital. I will also cover some essential investment vehicles you need to know about, such as real estate, securities, commodities, traditional currency, digital currency, and more. Finally, I will cover how wealthy families use estate planning tools like wills & trust to protect their assets, avoid taxes and create lasting wealth across multiple generations.

And here is why: *most people will work their entire lives, only to struggle in retirement.*

You want to read this book because you want a prosperous life for yourself and your children. Our planet has so much wealth and so many resources, yet most of it is controlled by a handful of the population. It is essential to understand why some people have great wealth that transcends generations, others are comfortable and can securely retire, and others will ultimately struggle their entire life. This concept is explained by the 5/15/80 percent wealth rule.

The first group is the 5 percent, the population of people who can create multigenerational wealth over time. These are the people who will create a system that passes wealth on to their children. The 15 percent refers to the middle-class population, who will be comfortable and create moderate wealth. (It is important to note that while many will live a comfortable middle-class life during their working years, many will not adequately prepare for their retirement years.) The 15 percent group is distinguished by being able to retire without assistance, although they will not create multigenerational wealth or pass down much to future generations like the 5 percent.

Finally, the 80 percent refers to the rest of the population. The 80 percent will need help from the government or will be heavily dependent on children or other family members to help them when they retire or can no longer work full-time. Most would agree that they want to be in the 5 percent or at least the 15 percent when they retire.

This book provides practical knowledge to help you take action, develop the discipline, and create a strategy to be a part of the 5 percent or the 15 percent. You don't want to die poor. And I can help you.

Your Guide to
Building Prosperity & Wealth

Chapter One
Mind Your Business!

"Small shifts in your thinking, and small changes in your energy, can lead to massive alteration of your results" (Michel, 2013). Since mindset is one of the foundational components of prosperity and economic stability, the next chapter will focus on developing a wealth mindset.

When I say *mind your business*, I mean a few things. First of all, it literally means to mind your business—focus on your goals and don't worry about what others are doing. You shouldn't do things for attention—never compare yourself to others, and don't waste valuable time but instead remain focused on creating the future you desire for yourself and your family.

Also, I want you to focus on the word *mind.* According to the Webster's dictionary, the definition of mind is as follows: the element of a person that enables them to be aware of the world and their experiences, to think, and to feel; the faculty of consciousness and thought; a person's intellect.

What you should take away from this is that you should be spending your time expanding your awareness of yourself and the universe around you and gaining knowledge that can be applied to creating economic value and forging a wealth mindset.

Wealth Mindset

What is a wealth mindset? It is a thought pattern that creates habits, behaviors, and processes that lead to a view of the world from a perspective of abundance, a disciplined approach to spending, and a focus on economic value creation, along with constantly identifying ways to make money work for you.

This means being laser-focused on forward-looking goals while investing in your knowledge about how money can work for you and taking incremental actions to improve your financial future. It is pivotal to understand that before you can be successful in building your financial portfolio, you must focus on building a wealth mindset. There are six principles to master for transforming your thinking to that of a wealth mindset. Master these principles to begin your journey to financial freedom and the life you desire—abundance thinking, learning to earn, investing in yourself, time is wealth, it's deeper than money, and focused discipline.

#1: Abundance Thinking

The first principle, abundance thinking, will transform how you see the world and undoubtedly will change how you get out of bed each morning once it is applied to your lifestyle. Abundance thinking is a realization that there is room for you to achieve your goals and that most of the barriers you create are only in your head and should not stop your pursuit of excellence.

It is the opposite of scarcity thinking, which causes us to believe that we cannot achieve our goals because only certain people are capable; we don't have the time or the constant fear that some seen or unseen entity is going to take things away.

Scarcity thinking manifests itself in many different ways, and I come across this mindset quite a bit in my coaching business. I once had a client, Samantha, who was in quite a funk about her career progression. She came to me because she wanted to get promoted to the next management level at her technology company. Instead of focusing on what she could do to be in the best situation for promotions, she was overly focused on those who were getting promoted before her.

She had been with the company for four years and was a high performer and expert in her field, which is why she had been recruited to join the firm in the first place. She described to me that the only people getting promoted had established relationships and also shared other mind stories explaining why she wasn't likely to be selected for promotion.

I asked her what was preventing her from establishing relationships, building her professional brand with key decision-makers, and whether she had expressed interest in higher roles to her leadership and those of influence. She had not attempted to make additional connections or even put her name in the hat for the position!

She was so consumed with thinking about barriers that her mindset became a barrier. Once she was able to change her perspective with mindfulness exercises on abundance thinking, she took the action needed to achieve her goal. Abundance thinking dictates that there is room for her growth, even if it means finding that room somewhere else. Now, she is the success and paycheck that comes with her promotion to management!

People with abundance thinking know that their gifts will make room for them, even if they have to build their own building. They don't wait to be tapped on the shoulder; they are constantly preparing for the opportunities they want and knocking on doors proactively to secure those opportunities.

Develop abundance thinking by practicing writing down bold, realistic goals you want to accomplish and taking daily actions to achieve those goals. Next, practice visualizing yourself achieving those goals in the future each morning. Finally, write down positive statements affirming you are accomplishing the desired outcome, and be sure to remove any passive words. Record those statements and play them back to yourself while you sleep or during a quiet moment.

#2: Learning to Earn

Did you know that a common attribute of individuals with self-made wealth is that they constantly read and seek knowledge to improve their lives? For example, Bill Gates reads approximately fifty books per year, and Oprah Winfrey selects one book every month for her famous book club. Reading to secure knowledge is a fundamental building block to the wealth mindset.

I started building this muscle very early. One of the first books I read was *Rich Dad, Poor Dad*, written by Robert Kiyosaki. This book changed my life, teaching me that you don't need to earn a high income to be wealthy (although it helps). In the book, Kiyosaki discusses his poor dad, who is his biological father. His father believed that the key to life was studying hard, getting good grades, and ultimately finding a well-paying job. However, despite being well-educated and following this principle, his father was not financially successful.

In contrast, his rich dad—a friend's father—also worked hard but believed in financial education. So, he spent his time learning all he could about how money works and making sure money worked for him even when he was sleeping.

Like the rich dad in Kiyosaki's book, you must equip yourself with the knowledge to build your fortune. One of the easiest ways to get started with acquiring the knowledge needed for building wealth is by reading books! However, keep in mind that successful people don't just read anything—they are very selective about the books or content they consume, mainly reading material that educates them rather than for entertainment purposes.

According to the book *Rich Habits*, written by Thomas C. Corley, the type of books that people read with annual incomes greater than $160,000 and a net worth of three million dollars or more revolve around the categories of education, self-improvement, and success. Similar to the need to eat healthy foods and exercise our bodies for peak physical performance, we must feed our minds with useful information and practice habits that enhance our ways of thinking.

You might also ask, "If learning is so important, why do we hear so many stories of currently wealthy people dropping out of school?" First off, this is more like the exception than the rule, and most people would likely not have the same successful outcome without education. The point is that while they may have departed from formal education, they never stopped learning, expanding their mind, and growing in their craft.

Suppose you wonder what topics and books would expand your knowledge. In that case, I recommend reading books that help build your discipline and focus, like *Atomic Habits* by James Clear, *The 7 Habits of Highly Effective People* by Stephen Covey, and *Think & Grow Rich* by Napoleon Hill—these books will help reinforce the wealth mindset.

Also, I suggest books about economics and finance, like *PowerNomics* by Claud Anderson, *The Color of Money* by Mehrsa Baradaran, and *The Millionaire Next Door* by Thomas Stanley. These books are a great primer to help you learn more about money and economics.

For those curious about books explicitly focused on investments, I recommend reading *Rental Property Investing* by Brandon Turner, *The Intelligent Investor* by Benjamin Graham, and *Barron's Finance & Investment Handbook*. These are great reference books about two of the most crucial wealth-generation assets, real estate, and stocks.

Additionally, I recommend exploring books about entrepreneurship, like *Side Hustle Millionaire* by Tony Whatley, *Starting a Business QuickStart Guide* by Ken Colwell, and *Mind Your Business* by Ilana Griffo. My final book suggestions include stories of inspiration, like *Black Fortunes* by Shomari Wills, *The Wealth Choice* by Dennis Kimbro, and *Can't Hurt Me* by David Goggins. I recommend these books because they provide good insight into wealth creation and business foundations and support and reinforce some of the topics covered in this book.

#3: Investing in Yourself

The following principle of the wealth mindset is to invest in yourself. Investing in yourself is one of the most important things you can do to improve your success on the road to wealth and financial freedom.

Investing in yourself includes investing in new skills in both personal and professional development. It also includes activities like hiring a fitness and career coach to improve your health and career outlook to meet the rigors of your daily life. Also, it may consist of investing time and resources in increasing your skill set and capabilities. These skills can help you improve your earning potential with a new job, start your new business venture, or take a course to teach you how to invest in stocks to grow your financial portfolio. For example, one of my clients, David, was interested in moving from a role in sales to a dream role in multicultural marketing. So, he enrolled in a program I offer called "Best Success Career Cohort," which helps mid-level employees grow their careers by teaching them tools and techniques to increase their professional brand, networking skills, and more. After two months of group training and individual coaching, David successfully pursued and interviewed for the role of multicultural marketing. His small investment in knowledge and development led to the desired role and a nice salary increase!

A couple of great resources to help you invest in yourself include reading the book *7 Habits of Highly Effective* People by Stephen Covey to get some practical tools on self-development to increase your productivity and taking courses on platforms such as Udemy, Courser or LinkedIn Learning. If you have a larger budget to spend on your development, organizations such as the General Assembly have great courses on topics ranging from digital marketing to software development. Doing those things listed above may be a means to increase your skill set to gain higher income roles.

Also, investing in yourself means paying yourself first from every paycheck before you loan money to others, spend cash on entertainment, or even pay bills. Putting some of your money aside is imperative to fund your financial freedom. This will allow you to invest in assets like stock, cash-flowing businesses, and side hustles to improve your earnings. We will cover this topic in more detail in Chapter Four.

To facilitate paying yourself first, I suggest setting up reoccurring payments into a savings account, a mutual fund, or a retirement account so that it automatically happens. Some companies allow you to deduct money from your paycheck into investment accounts before receiving it, which may be tax-deductible.

Finally, you should look at your 9-to-5 job as a short-term solution to the long-term goal of creating financial freedom. Unless you enjoy working for others, you should be leveraging your full-time job to pay for your freedom.

For example, freedom could mean building up your investments and retirement portfolio to support retiring early. Freedom also means putting money away to start a business to generate enough additional income to replace what you make working each day. To achieve independence, you must quickly learn that the poor and middle class work for money, while the wealthy work to control their time by making their money work for them. In reality, the actual currency of wealth is the control of one's time.

#4: Time Is Wealth

Time is undoubtedly your most important asset, and money is just a means to free up your time to do as you please. Unfortunately, many highly-paid individuals are held captive by their wealth because how they earn their money doesn't give them time to focus on the things they value.

While trading time for money is virtually unavoidable for most people starting out, I believe the primary objective for us all should be to create time by creating income-generating assets that work with limited to no interaction from the owner.

The good news is that this type of income is increasingly accessible to the average individual right now. For example, in 2020, seeing a need for an e-commerce company that ships snacks and activities to working parents at home with kids because of COVID, I created *Snack 'n Fun Box*. While the business required much of my time at first, less than two years later, I was able to automate this business so that packing and shipping are completed by a third party, and marketing is automated—allowing my business to become essentially passive.

We are amid a new revolution—the digital revolution. With the invention of the internet, it is now easier than ever to make money while you sleep by leveraging technology and automation tools. You can leverage several ideas to make money while you sleep or, in the famous words of Representative Maxine Waters, to "reclaim your time."

One option to earn some passive income is to start a blog. It is inexpensive, only requiring leveraging a hosting site such as GoDaddy or WordPress to get started. However, *content is king*, so make sure you have great content with mass-appeal topics. A great way to determine if a topic is popular is to leverage Keyword Trends, a tool that Google offers to provide insight into the popularity of particular words. In addition, you will need to leverage social media or word of mouth to drive traffic to your site, as people may not know you exist otherwise. The key to making money on a blog is to create a large following to secure sponsors or sell advertisements on your site.

Another option is to create an e-commerce business to sell products online. For example, consider selling beauty, health, and consumable products that people frequently use. However, to stand out, identify niche products that are harder for customers to find but that you can provide in a one-stop shop. For example, Holigong is an online store that specializes in holiday décor. They have everything you need for those Christmas and Halloween celebrations and more for customers who love to decorate their homes for those special occasions. There are several ways to do this: you can leverage platforms such as Etsy, Shopify, or Weebly to transact with customers or work with e-commerce brands like Walmart, eBay, and Amazon to sell your product through their platform by creating a seller's account.

Another way to earn money while you sleep is through royalties. Earning royalties often requires talent such as acting, singing, writing music, or writing a book to capture residual income from your intellectual assets. This requires licensing your intellectual property to a third party for a fee or percentage of every sale they make using it. For example, I have created several coloring and activity books sold on Amazon and Barnes & Noble, for which I receive royalty payments each time a book is sold. Inventions also fall into this category; this is an excellent idea if you are an engineer or able to develop a product you can license to corporations. In my work in mergers and acquisitions, I witness inventors make considerable amounts of money from the licensing of technology and selling that technology to larger companies that want to acquire intellectual property.

A third option is investing in stocks, one of the oldest and most proven ways to earn money while you sleep. Stock investing requires learning how the stock market works to leverage tools like E*Trade, Fidelity, or other investment vehicles in trading your cash for ownership of a portion of a company called shares. As the company performs financially, there is an expectation that the value of each share will appreciate, thus growing your money. The key is buying when the stock price has gone down and there is evidence that the stock price is undervalued, which can be tricky. Additionally, many stocks pay shareholders' annual or quarterly dividends (small cash earnings). We cover this topic in more detail in Chapter Seven.

Real estate investing is another favorite vehicle for earning money while you sleep. You can purchase a property to rent out for more significant than your monthly mortgage payment. You make money from the difference in rent and mortgage payments. Additionally, the renter is essentially paying the mortgage payment and loan interest, helping you build equity in the property. Meanwhile, the value of your investment increases if you purchase in an area with appreciating home values. There are other innovative ways to earn income in real estate, such as subleasing on platforms like Airbnb, which allow you to rent your home out to vacationers/visitors looking for an alternative to a hotel.

#5: It's Deeper than Money

Let's face it, money itself is a shallow motivator: the blind pursuit of money can lead you to build a glamorous prison around you or send you to jail. We all can name several wealthy individuals—from Bernie Madoff to Allen Stanford—in prison because of bad business practices and corrupt behavior, such as creating a Ponzi scheme to steal money from unsuspecting people. To avoid these pitfalls, you need motivation that will give you a more profound reason to succeed because the wealth journey isn't easy.

Ask any entrepreneur who has created a successful business how many times they have wanted to quit or what kept them going. And the answer is likely that they wanted to quit many times, as money wasn't the primary motivator to their success.

When I was working on my M.B.A., I had the opportunity to speak to several successful CEOs and entrepreneurs and ask them what kept them motivated to achieve their professional success. Surprisingly, none of the answers were centered around financial gain.

Instead, the answers were focused on the person's legacy, family, or making life better for others. Whether it's creating a legacy, freedom, or charity, your reason must be driven by something more profound than the superficial. Therefore, you must spend time figuring out your *why*. This principle is arguably one of the essential principles of the wealth mindset.

To identify your *why*, ask yourself the following questions: what are the things you can do to make other people's lives better? What do you want your legacy to be when you are no longer alive? What activities can you do for hours without noticing or feeling like you're doing a chore? Ultimately, you have to be content with your life beyond simply having lots of money. If you genuinely want to succeed in your craft, chase excellence, not money! Finally, you must possess a deep connection to your *why*—that your purpose for creating your empire is driven internally by something deeper than materialistic items, or you will find yourself unfulfilled. One of my business partners in real estate owns a successful bakery; when he and his wife started their business, it was very difficult, with many tough years where they wanted to give up. However, they wanted to create a life of freedom so that they could travel and leave an inheritance for their son. This gave them the perseverance to weather the stormy years when business was tough, and they needed to grow their clientele.

Now they have a thriving business that provides them the resources to fund incredible beach vacations surrounded by clear blue water and the lifestyle they always dreamed about.

#6: Focused Discipline

The final principle is focused discipline. This section focuses on increasing your ability to follow through, enabling you to fulfill your goals. Let's begin by defining both focus and discipline: focus requires training yourself to do something in a controlled and habitual way, and discipline means studying or learning, training, and applying a system of standards. Therefore, I define focused discipline as the ability to have laser focus on a goal while leveraging a system to consistently and methodically develop the capabilities to reach that goal.

We all have a relative, neighbor, or childhood associate who has been telling us for several years how they are going to start a business or pursue some other goal. Yet, they have never put any meaningful effort into creating or investing in the skills/tools necessary to achieve the desired goal. This inability to pursue a goal is likely due to a lack of discipline.

There are also individuals who are good at starting something but have never actually completed anything. Again, this is due to a lack of focus.

Five practical steps you can implement to help create a more focused discipline are as follows:

1. Write down all the goals you want to accomplish and rank them in importance; choose the top three. The truth is you can only really focus on a few things to complete at any given time. Additionally, your goals should be simple, measurable, achievable, realistic, and time-bound—for example, if you want to open a bakery. Another example of a good goal would be, "I want to start a t-shirt printing business in three months on Shopify. I will spend one hour on this business each day and achieve my first sale during my first week, post-launch."

2. Write down your goals and reflect on them daily to keep them top of mind.

3. Schedule time every day or on a consistent cadence to work on those goals. For example, you could wake up early and schedule one hour each day before you have your morning coffee. It doesn't have to be a lot of time, but you should increase it as needed. The point is to start developing a habit and discipline to work on the goal.

4. Develop a visible way to track or mark your progress toward these goals. For example, you could use a journal or a whiteboard in your office or bedroom. While you should write down an action plan that aligns with each of these goals, what you are focused on here is building a habit of discipline.

5. Schedule time to periodically reflect on how you can improve and get feedback from others. Reflecting will allow you to determine if you are making progress and whether you need to make any changes.

The point is to spend meaningful time working toward accomplishing your goals, whether learning, reflecting, planning, or taking practical steps. It is vital to start and keep moving forward, as people will often spend too much time in the preparation stage and never take any meaningful action.

Another essential aspect of focused discipline is not waiting for things to feel right. You must get used to stepping outside of your comfort zone and getting the ball rolling. Stepping out on faith will require changing your routine and gradually building your endurance for focused discipline, undoubtedly leading to success.

I recommend reading two terrific books to help you develop the habits needed for focused discipline and forging your wealth mindset: *Atomic Habits* and *7 Habits of Highly Effective People*. As Dr. Claude Richards, author of *PowerNomics*, said, "Focused discipline requires breaking those 'badass' habits."

For example, this means creating a budget and waiting until you have established an emergency fund before buying that Louis Vuitton bag. The goal should be to be wealthy and not look wealthy by wearing all your money.

From a financial standpoint, a critical foundation to wealth creation is generating a monthly and yearly budget to help you allocate where your money is spent that aligns with your saving, investing, and personal goals. Some great tools make this virtually easy and seamless, such as Mint from Intuit, PocketGuard, or Honeydue for budgeting with a partner. I prefer Mint since it allows me to integrate all my accounts, spending, and financial goals in one view. It even calculates your net worth and incorporates credit scoring. The point is to find what works best for you.

In the next chapter, you will learn about handling and managing your finances with business industry secrets and savviness.

Chapter Summary/Key Takeaways

This chapter explores the necessary components in thinking about your financial future. The wealth mindset has several principles to help you restructure how you view money and what steps you take to strengthen this mindset within you.

The wealth mindset principles are abundance thinking, learning to earn, investing in yourself, time is wealth, it's deeper than money, and focused discipline.

It can be challenging to shift your mindset; however, if you follow the advice and guidance outlined in each of these principles, you will get closer to achieving the financial and career success you yearn for and strive for daily.

Be sure to keep your eyes on your goals, even when things get tough. Use the tools mentioned earlier to make yourself accountable in your quest to be financially sound.

Chapter Two
Being CEO of Y.O.U.

Being the CEO of Y.O.U. (Your Own Universe) means managing your personal affairs and life, to a certain extent, like a business. In this section, I will teach you how to manage your personal finances like that of a company. Because, let's face it: if you don't take control of your life, no one is going to step in and do it for you.

I'm not saying it's easy or will not require some discipline, but these lessons, along with the practical application, can allow you to take control of your future and truly become your own CEO.

Budgeting like a Pro

Budgets are the foundation of money management and a building block to wealth creation and your first step in this process. However, I want to change the way you think about budgeting because it is not the handcuffs you might think it is—in reality, it is one of the first keys to unlocking your freedom, and we all want freedom.

Also, you can consider a budget as your "business plan." Every company has some type of business plan to get them started and help them make decisions. In a subsequent chapter, I will discuss how to start a business and create a business plan in greater detail. In its most simple form, a budget allows you to know what income you have coming in versus how much you are spending. This will help you have the focused discipline for wealth creation mentioned in this book's building your wealth mindset section.

The first step in creating a budget is to approximate your income and expenses for the year so that you have a plan for your money. Looking at your old bank statements is a wonderful way to get a baseline on what and how much you spend. You should break your budget into monthly buckets so that you can frequently track it and make adjustments within a reasonable timeframe. Make sure you schedule time on your calendar each month to review the budget with your household and yourself to drive accountability or celebrate achieving your goals.

After creating a budget, set yearly financial goals around how much you plan to earn, save, and invest. Then, be sure to determine the expenses you have that can be reduced or eliminated. For example, do you need to buy new shoes every paycheck, or do you need to eat out every single day? Perhaps prioritizing new brakes for your car is more important than popping bottles at the club,

Now, I'm not saying you have to go without your wants and desires completely, but you have to plan for them and put yourself on a path that increases your current ability to afford them. Ask yourself, would you rather look wealthy or *be* wealthy because you made the right decisions early?

Also, if you don't like how much money you have left after expenses, then set some goals to increase your income with additional income streams. Be sure to read the section on multiple income streams to help you do this. After reading this, you might ask yourself, why is budgeting necessary? Well, if you don't want to be broke, just getting by or working hard all your life, it might be wise to make short-term sacrifices for long-term positive outcomes.

If budgeting seems daunting, there are some apps out there that integrate with your bank to help you create and track a budget, such as Simplifi by Quicken and Mint by Intuit. I love using Mint, but do some research to determine what works best for you. I also use a spreadsheet from time to time so that I can play with different income and expense scenarios.

Understanding Personal Financial Statements

Next, let's talk about personal financial statements. Every well-run corporation is managed according to its financial statements. You can look at your financial statements as a map of your money. Like a map, if you don't know where you are currently, it isn't easy to understand how to get to your destination. On this journey, the destination is the freedom of wealth, and your current location is the present state of your finances.

There are three corporate financial statements for corporations that are created each year to measure company performance. They are income, balance sheet, and cash flow. For the sake of your personal finances, we will focus on two that best apply to an individual and are directly tied to how you manage cash. These statements are your *personal cash flow statement* and *personal balance sheet.*

First, let's talk about the cash flow statement. The cash flow statement measures your cash inflows (money you bring in) versus cash outflows (money you spend). I suggest measuring cash flow monthly and yearly. Your cash inflow includes cash coming into your households, such as your salary from your job, income from side hustles and businesses you created, or dividend payments from investments. Cash inflows would also include money earned from assets sold.

On the other hand, cash outflow includes expenses or the short-term portion of liabilities. For example, common cash outflows would be rent or mortgage payments, utility bills, groceries, car payments, gas/fuel, and entertainment expenses.

You want to measure the difference between your cash inflows and outflows to determine whether your net cash flow is positive or negative and to what extent.

Net cash flow is simply subtracting all cash outflows from cash inflows. Your cash flow statement goes hand in hand with your budget. Your budget is your plan, and the cash flow statement represents how well you execute the plan to manage your finances.

Many companies and celebrities who make substantial cash have found themselves in financial trouble. After all, they didn't pay attention to how much cash was left over each month because they spent more money than what they were making. Failure to understand cash flow led them into bankruptcy. For example, Mike Tyson earned approximately $400M during his boxing career, and despite earning huge sums of money, by 2003, he had declared bankruptcy.

Next, let's talk about the balance sheet because this will help you understand your net worth and is necessary for creating your wealth strategy.

The balance sheet consists of assets, liabilities, and owner equity or net worth. Let's first talk about *assets*, as this is often misunderstood. Assets are not just things you own—an asset is something that creates value, whether it generates income, appreciates over time, or can do both. If it doesn't make money, it doesn't make sense.

Some examples of assets are income-generating real estate property, revenue-producing land, inventory, unpaid revenue from others that are likely to be paid, and equipment you own with a resale value. It also includes intellectual property such as books you have written, royalties on music or content, social media pages generating advertisement revenue, a business you own or has an equity stake in. Other appreciating belongings, such as artwork and antiques, have been appraised and certified to have cash value.

On the other hand, a *liability* takes money from you that you are obligated to pay. Therefore, a new home is not necessarily an asset because you have an obligation to pay a mortgage. However, the equity that results after you have paid off a portion of it has a cash value, making it an asset since you could do a cash-out refinance to utilize the cash value.

In Chapter Six, I will talk about real estate and how you can use it in your wealth creation journey. It is also essential to distinguish between liabilities and expenses. Expenses are cash spent each month for you to operate your way of living.

I categorize expenses as necessary and unnecessary. The necessary expenses, for example, are things like groceries, shelter, and transportation. Some expenses support assets and are associated with revenue-producing activities within necessary expenses. I call these types of necessary expenses *productive* expenses. Productive expenses include things like software subscriptions for your business or computers.

On the other hand, I think of liabilities as an expense associated with assets, like a loan used to purchase equipment for your business. Liabilities are not necessarily bad—in fact, they are necessary. For example, if you don't have a large amount of cash, you may need to take a loan to purchase revenue-generating assets.

In actuality, many wealthy people will secure debt to invest in revenue-producing assets while keeping their cash for a rainy day or as collateral. Basically, it is sometimes better to use other people's money than your own. Although many popular wealth advisors will tell you to be debt-free, debt can be a valuable tool to increase your earnings. Think about it—how many growing companies have absolutely no debt? Not many. The key is understanding that your debt should be a liability associated with revenue-producing assets and how much debt it makes sense for you or your business to carry. Some liabilities include mortgage payments on any property you possess, student loans, personal loans for your business, salaries you pay to employees, income tax payable, payments for merchandise from customers in advance of them receiving any inventory, and equipment for businesses bought on credit.

We focus on buying income-producing assets and getting as much value out of them while keeping our liabilities low with managing a company. Essentially, avoid creating debt for things unrelated to revenue-producing assets, such as buying a big-screen TV or securing store credit to go on a shopping spree.

In the next chapter, we talk about the areas of owner's equity and net worth. The owner's equity in a corporation is essentially the owner's right to the assets of a business. For you, it's what's left over after you have subtracted all the liabilities from the assets. So, think of net worth and owner's equity being the same thing from a personal finance standpoint. In the next section on personal finance ratios, I will talk about how to calculate your net worth and how to think about it more.

Chapter Summary/Key Takeaways

This chapter explores the critical components of viewing your personal finances the same way businesses view their finances. Being CEO of Y.O.U entails budgeting your expenses and understanding your personal financial statements. To understand your financial statements, you must know about the personal balance sheet and personal cash flow statement—tools that can assist you in seeing your finances more clearly.

You have to understand where you have been to envision where you want to go. Knowing about your cash inflows and outflows, liabilities, and assets can get you on the path toward financial freedom. Recognizing where your money is spent should guide you in how you choose to spend your money daily.

Using the wealth mindset and knowing how you spend your money will guide you further down the road to wealth creation. Evaluate whether your spending is getting you closer or further away from your goal, then become disciplined in how that money is spent. In the next chapter, you will learn about measuring your financial health through ratios and measures.

Chapter Three
Checking Your Financial Health

When managing your finances like a company, you must have quick and straightforward ways to measure your financial health. Every day, corporations leverage what is known as financial ratios to do just this.

Financial ratios are simple calculations used to evaluate a company's performance and make decisions for the business based on a standard set of measurements and rules of thumb. Similarly, you can use personal financial ratios to help you evaluate your financial health and make decisions for your financial portfolio. These measures show you a snapshot of your financial health using two key numbers regarding your money and can help you decide how much you are spending each month, how much you should be saving, and how much debt you should be holding at any given time. I've included a few personal financial ratios below that I think everyone should know.

Knowing Your Net Worth

You can view your net worth as a financial report card. The first measure is to evaluate your personal balance sheet (see Chapter Two for instructions on how to compile this). Net worth is your total wealth, which considers your financial assets and liabilities. Ideally, the number of assets you own should exceed your liabilities or debt obligations.

I use tools like Intuit's Mint, a personal financial management website, and a mobile app to track all of my assets and liabilities into one view to calculate my net worth and view my personal balance sheet.

The first time I started tracking my net worth, it was negative, even though I made considerable money. With awareness, discipline, and a wealth strategy, I improved my net worth significantly to nearly half a million in less than five years.

It's important to note that net worth and cash flow go hand in hand. Since cash flow feeds everything else, it is one of the most important concepts to understand. That is why you should not look at any ratio in isolation.

The formula for net worth = total assets - total liabilities. You may have a negative net worth, but don't let that discourage you—once you know your status, set goals to help you increase your net worth. Improving your net worth means either decreasing your liabilities or increasing your assets. The good news is that this book will give you some practical tips to do just that!

Debt-to-Assets Ratio

The next measure that aligns with your personal balance sheet is the debt-to-assets ratio. It measures how much debt you have relative to your assets and is a good indicator of whether you should pay off some debt before taking on new obligations.

As mentioned in the section on the personal balance sheet, some debt is not necessarily bad if it is helping you to grow. However, a poor debt-to-asset ratio could limit whether a bank will lend you money for your new venture. In most cases, the rule of thumb is to not exceed 50 percent debt-to-asset ratio; however, 10 percent is an ideal goal to achieve.

Debt is important to manage because your credit score factors the amount of debt you use relative to the amount you can access. The formula for debt-to-assets ratio = total liabilities / total assets.

Investment Assets to Total Assets Ratio

Another ratio important to personal wealth management is the comparison of investment assets to total assets. This ratio compares liquid assets, such as cash, and near cash assets, such as investments in stocks, bonds, mutual funds, or other investments that can be converted into cash against total assets. Conversely, illiquid assets are such things as real estate or other assets that would take much longer to convert to cash. Therefore, 20% of your assets should be liquid. This level of liquidity would allow you access to money for emergencies or investment opportunities—the formula for investment assets to total assets = liquid assets / total assets.

Savings Ratio

In 2008, the financial crisis hit me like a ton of bricks. I recently started working for a manufacturing company being responsible for supply chain management. The company was hitting record numbers when a financial crisis hit, reducing demand for our product. As a management team, we decided we all would take furloughs or unpaid time off to avoid a reduction in force.

My cash flow was immediately reduced. Fortunately, I had set up an emergency account for times such as this. While it was painful, I might have lost my home or been unable to pay my bills without an emergency account.

The savings ratio is essential to help you be prepared financially from a cash standpoint. It indicates the amount of cash or cash equivalents an individual puts aside as savings for the future compared with gross income. Gross income includes salary, proceeds from your business or side hustle, bonuses, etc.

Most advisors say you should save 20% of your income if possible. The formula for savings ratio = savings / gross income. It may be challenging to save significant amounts when starting; therefore, start with an incremental savings goal and build from there.

You should aim toward three savings levels in your savings strategy. Level one is to save $1,000–$5,000 for an emergency event such as a car repair or traveling for a family emergency. The next level is establishing an emergency fund for a job loss or a longer-term crisis scenario—your emergency fund should include enough funds to cover three to six months of expenses. The third level is anything above six months, where you are saving your money in cash-equivalent investments for higher interest investments, ventures, or reducing debt obligations.

While *cash is undoubtedly king*, you should ensure your cash is working for you. Any cash beyond six months should not just sit in a savings account but eventually be transferred to longer-term investments or income-generating assets.

The Financial Freedom Ratio

This final ratio measures your ability to quit your full-time job and reclaim your time to focus on what interests you. The freedom ratio means having income coming in from sources outside of your primary source of income, including passive and side hustle income.

Here, there are three primary levels to achieve. Level one is having some amount of income beyond your primary job. Also, you should start with a goal of saving 10% of your income. Level two is having enough non-primary income (passive income, side hustle, business, etc.) to cover your expenses. Level three is having enough additional income that replaces your salary at 100% or more. Level three is an important savings milestone giving you the security of having enough income to cover yourself should you lose your job. The financial freedom ratio = non-primary income / primary income.

In the next chapter, you will learn about multiple ways to earn income and how doing so will get you even closer to the financial freedom you seek.

Chapter Summary/Key Takeaways

This chapter explains how to evaluate your financial health using various financial ratios and measures.

Using your personal balance sheet, you can calculate your net worth, debt-to-asset ratio, investment assets-to-total assets ratio, savings ratio, and financial freedom ratio. Knowing how much you are worth and how you can either add to that by saving or investing will allow you to see the steps you should take to achieve your financial freedom goals.

In addition, understanding how much of your income goes toward debt can help you eliminate unnecessary debts, which in turn, makes your financial future more robust.

These tools will allow you to gain a bigger and better picture of your financial status and lead you down the route to your desired financial goals.

Chapter Four
Creating Multiple Income Streams

Most financial gurus will focus on helping you get out of debt and give you a regimen for creating a budget to manage your cash more effectively. While managing the money you already have is foundational and especially important to financial freedom, most people simply don't make enough money or have enough income to achieve what they want to accomplish financially.

If you're going to increase your discretionary cash flow, you will either reduce your expenses, increase your cash inflow, or both. I often work with professionals who want to get promoted and earn higher wages in my coaching business. Identifying ways to make more money is critical to increasing cash flow since most of us will begin with our job as the first and only income source.

Another essential concept for wealth creation is setting a goal to create multiple income streams beyond your primary income source. One of the apparent reasons for creating multiple income streams is that you make more money, which puts you closer to achieving the financial freedom ratio, potentially giving you enough income to replace what you make in your day job. Creating multiple income streams also offers you financial protection should you lose your job and contribute to meeting your retirement savings goal early.

One of the first lessons I learned in investments is to diversify your portfolio to help mitigate risk from one company or industry; the same principle of diversification applies to the income we depend on each month to live and pay bills. I can assure you that your confidence at work, or in general, will undoubtedly increase when you are not entirely dependent on your day job to survive. When implemented correctly, this can effectively reduce risk.

One important concept to remember is the principle of focused discipline. Be sure to apply focused discipline by getting one or two streams stable before you get started with new streams, as it's easy to lose focus. Another valued concept is identifying streams you can automate or allow you to leverage others to do the nonessential work that will free up your time. Sir Richard Branson is famous for creating successful businesses and finding brilliant people to run them for him. Identifying competent people to lead his various organizations allows him to strategically focus on his entire portfolio and have a broader reach as he grows his empire.

Also, multiple income streams do not have to be completely disparate businesses or concepts. The most successful way to achieve this is to ensure that each stream is related or adjacent to the previous. Focusing on closely related ventures will make it easier to focus, operationalize, and create efficiency that frees up your time.

For example, if you have a t-shirt business, you could repurpose some designs to create excellent artistic journals or notepads. That effectively is using the same effort to monetize additional streams of income.

I often advise my small business clients or mentees to create an ecosystem when developing multiple income streams. For example, suppose a client is a thought leader in healthcare consulting. In that case, they could leverage their knowledge to create an on-demand course for individuals who want to gain some of their expertise beyond consulting engagements. They could also leverage some of the content they have created from their course and experience with clients to create a book that can be sold online or in bookstores. How does this become an ecosystem? It becomes one when each of the streams supports and links to each other.

Here is a scenario to illustrate this concept more clearly. Because the client is an expert in healthcare consulting, people are more likely to purchase their book, which leads to more book sales. Also, when people discover their book and the fact that they are publishing in this space, they will be more attractive for consulting contracts with companies.

Additionally, they may be able to leverage their position during consulting engagements to interest people in taking the course they offer. Finally, the book and course could lead to paid speaking engagements. In this scenario, each income stream is related and supports the other streams, making them more profitable than they may have been if they were separate. Also, because each stream leverages similar content and expertise, it doesn't put as much strain on the entrepreneur as dissimilar streams would.

Types of Income

There are three categories of income—earned, portfolio, and passive. Earned income is what you make from working or trading your time in exchange for money, whether you receive a salary, hourly rate, or consulting fees. Earned income is taxed at the highest rate, ranging between 10% and 37%. The benefit of earned income is that it is the easiest to obtain for most people—you simply need to find a job. The downside is that earned income is limited to the number of hours you are physically capable of working or based on the number of hours your employer allows you to work.

Portfolio income is the money you earn on the gains or increases to the money you make in investing, like stocks, bonds, real estate, precious metals, and artwork/antiquities. Capital gains tax on portfolio income is generally less than that of earned income, ranging from 0% to 20% depending on the assets, which may require consultation from an accountant. One great benefit to buying assets in this category is that gains can be offset by losses and are not subject to Medicare and social security taxes. Portfolio income is probably where most of the wealthiest people have grown their income, but it requires some learning to have the best outcome. It can also require more patience as some assets can take years or even decades to reach their maximum value. Nevertheless, this is a beautiful place to take some of the money you are saving from earned income to start building your future.

The third category is passive income, which is money you earn from things you create that don't require significant active involvement to gain money. For example, creating passive income would include creating and selling items such as books, income from an online course, or royalties from intellectual property that you created. For instance, in my business, Fun Media Designs, I was able to create passive income by creating several coloring books that provide me with passive income because I sell them at online retailers that print the products on demand when customers order them. Passive income also enjoys lower tax rates than earned income generally, but it is essential to leverage a licensed accountant to help you sort through the tax implications.

Passive income is one of the best sources of income because you can earn it while you sleep, with a limited amount of involvement, and it has lots of longevity that add up over time.

So why do you need to understand the various categories of income? So that it will help you create your wealth-building strategy and decide on which income types to leverage depending on the pros and cons as you create multiple income streams. You will likely want to have income types from all three initially but move to portfolio and passive as you get closer to financial freedom.

Leverage your earned income to *invest in yourself* by learning to invest in portfolio assets or passive income-producing assets like real estate and simple business models that run automatically or do not require a lot of your time. For example, you could leverage your earned income from your job as a nurse to create a blog site that attracts lots of viewers to make advertisement revenue. Or, it can be embedded with affiliate links for nursing-related products to earn passive income that you could subsequently use to invest in stocks or bonds. Then you can put that investment in your portfolio income so that you can use it after you retire.

In the next chapter, you will learn about starting your own business and the tools you will need to make this dream come true.

Chapter Summary/Key Takeaways

This chapter focuses on multiple income streams and how they can fund your financial freedom. The three types of income, earned, passive, and portfolio, are all legitimate and intelligent ways of strengthening your financial health.

In the early stages of working toward financial freedom, you may use all three types, but you may discover that one or two ways may work better for you. Investing in stocks, creating an online course, or writing an e-book are just a few ways to generate more income streams for your personal finances.

Remember, try to keep the streams along the same lines so that you can maximize your earning potential. Your financial freedom goal may not solely depend on your full-time job, so having multiple income streams will get you to that freedom goal much quicker.

Chapter Five
Starting Your Own Business

One of the best ways to gain freedom, create another income stream, and control your life is to start a business. I have started several companies to various degrees of success. My first business was simply selling clothes on eBay. I didn't conduct any research, nor did I have a plan which led to a failed business. Starting a business requires a lot of work, but you can create your next successful venture with a few steps. Whether you want to serve your famous wings by starting a food truck business, a personal training company, or an online store to sell t-shirts, the nuts and bolts are the same.

Developing the Idea

If you have been reading to this point, you know that I am a huge fan of starting a business. I'll start off with those people at the early stage without a solid idea to bring to life. If so, ask yourself a few questions, such as what do people say you do really well? Understanding what you do well may help you figure out a way you can monetize yourself.

Also, think of products you like or use—how could those products be improved or reach an underserved audience?

What are people's most complaints about the products you are familiar with and passionate about?

Another question to ask is, what is something you dislike doing? Then think of a way to automate or digitize it.

Next, you might have an idea of what product or service you want to provide but don't know whether it's a good idea. Whether you are in the pre-idea stage or ready with a complete business idea, the rest of this section will be for you.

It's of great importance to connect your idea with customer pain points to have the most success. Essentially, what problem does your idea solve for the customer? For example, if you decide to start a mobile carwash business, you may be solving the customer's pain point for not having enough time to stop by a traditional carwash.

Next, ask yourself who would benefit the most from your service or solution. The segment of the population that benefits the most from your service or product would be your potential customer target audience.

You can test your assumption by creating a survey or asking people you encounter about this benefit and how much they would be willing to pay. You can use platforms like Qualtrics and Survey Monkey to create a survey. Also, depending on your business, market research sites like Mintel might be helpful.

Perhaps your research determines that your potential target audience is working professionals who desire a clean car but are too busy to wash their car because of their hectic schedule. However, with a few more questions, you might discover that working women with children make up much of the target audience.

Also, search the internet to see if any data already exist—there are many organizations or trade groups that conduct research you might want to leverage to get a better idea of the market potential for this business. You must conduct research to assess the market to gauge how significant the opportunity is for your potential business from a demand and revenue perspective. It's probably not worth starting a business if only five people care about what you are offering.

Next, you want to research what competitors are doing or whether this is an untapped market ripe for the picking. Capture a list of competitors and information about them that you can use to compete with them, like pricing strategy, distribution, and weaknesses and shortcomings in their product offering. It's also wise to get an idea of how much competition exists. Starting a business in a saturated market may not make sense unless your product is significantly better or unique. What you have just conducted is called market research.

Drafting Your Business Plan

The next step is to use the research results you gathered during the idea phase about customer needs, competition, market potential, and any other poignant research from the previous stage to create a business plan. Your business plan should articulate what your company is about and what products or services it offers. You will also want to define who is your target customer and why you are best able to solve their problem. Finally, communicate the problem or pain point you are solving for this customer or customers if there are multiple segments.

The next thing to include in your business plan is information about the competitors already operating within your niche of business and the geography you are targeting. Be sure to include in your plan how you will differentiate yourself from those competitors. (Differentiation means addressing pain points that competition has not previously solved, unique product size and packaging, exclusive services, and marketing strategies.)

You will also need to include financial projections showing that you understand how significant the opportunity is and how many shares of the pie you can reasonably acquire over time, say, five years. When selling a product, include how many units you are projected to sell and a pricing strategy for your product offering. Calculating the number of units you expect to sell and multiplying this number by your desired selling price will provide you with a rough estimate of potential revenue.

You will also need to estimate all the considerable expenses incurred while operating this business. A significant category of expenses includes the following: salaries for you or any employees, marketing or selling fees, cost of goods or inventory-related cost from the sale of a physical item, costs associated with property and equipment you need to use to run your business, administrative costs such as legal and accounting fees, and taxes.

If you go to templates.office.com, you can find several business plan templates to leverage. The Small Business Association (SBA) also provides templates on its site. Many people will tell you to create a business plan with 30 to 50 pages, but a business plan shouldn't be longer than 15 pages. It depends on the complexity of the business you wish to start. Don't let writing a business plan stop you from getting started either—if you are struggling, capture the basics mentioned above and keep moving forward.

Deciding on a Legal Structure

As far as deciding on a legal structure, there are many you can choose from. The important thing is to do the proper research and consult a lawyer and accountant since there are many pros and cons, depending on the type of business you want to set up.

The most common business structures are sole proprietors, partnerships, corporations, or limited liability corporations. A sole proprietor is a business with just one owner who pays personal income tax on profits earned from the company. The main benefits of a sole proprietorship are the pass-through tax advantage, the ease of creation, and lower fees for creation and maintenance. The disadvantages of a sole proprietorship are the unlimited liability that goes beyond the business to the owner and the difficulty in getting capital funding.

Another option for the legal structure of your business is a partnership. A partnership means that two or more people are held personally liable as business owners, and all parties equally share legal and financial liability. The individuals are personally responsible for the debts the partnership takes on. Profits are also shared equally. Partnerships are a typical structure for accountants, lawyers, and consultants. A corporation is a separate legal entity that separates personal and company liability. You may want to consider forming, for example, S corporation, C corporation, or B corporation. Each type of corporation is subject to different guidelines.

Because a corporation is a separate entity from its owners, corporations can own property, assume liability, pay taxes, enter contracts, sue, and be sued like any individual. If you choose this route, you must separate your personal finances from the businesses to avoid tax headaches.

Lastly, an LLC is an extremely popular way to set up your business. The owners are not personally liable for the company's debts or liabilities in an LLC. LLCs are hybrid entities that combine the characteristics of a corporation with those of a partnership or sole proprietorship. I have generally used the limited liability corporation, or LLC, for my startup companies. There are many types of limited liability corporations to choose from; therefore, it is essential to evaluate the pros and cons of each.

Government, Taxes, and Other Administrative Tasks

Now that you have a viable business idea, a solid plan, and have decided on a specific business structure, you are ready to legitimize your business with the federal and state government. Each state has its own requirements, but most will require you to file an Articles of Incorporation with the Secretary of State, which is a document that includes your business name, business purpose, corporate structure, stock details, and other information about your company.

The first step in this process is to select a name that another company has not already used. Therefore, research and choose a name that makes sense for your business.

You may also need to create an operating agreement that outlines members' rights and obligations and how the company will operate financially and administratively. The operating agreement will be essential when opening bank accounts for your business. You can leverage services like LegalZoom to help create such documents, find a business attorney, or use another source for a template that fits your needs.

For operating in the state you file your business with, you will pay a fee to the Secretary of State each year to file an annual report. After that, you will go to the Internal Revenue Service's website and file for an EIN or Federal Employer Identification Number for federal taxes. An EIN is a unique nine-digit number assigned by the Internal Revenue Service to business entities operating in the United States for identification.

Also, depending on your business type and the location where you are operating, you may need to secure various business licenses. Again, please research to find out what is required for your area.

Financing Your Business

Most businesses will require financing, and most will start interacting with their own funds or small investments from friends and family. However, depending on the type of business endeavor, this can be enough to get started, and you can reinvest it into your business as it grows.

Another option is to take out a loan, which will depend on your credit rating and financial standing. Some banks will require you to have some history of revenue before they are willing to lend to you. Many banks will want to see your business plan, operating agreements, and financial statements from the business or owners before giving out a loan. You can contact your local bank or the SBA for loans or grants to help you get started.

Depending on your business, you may be able to attract investors. Investors will give you money for equity or shares of ownership in your company. Unlike a typical loan with an interest rate on which you make payments each month, you don't pay back the money or pay a fixed interest rate. Instead, investors buy fractional ownership of your business. When you sell your company, investors will be entitled to a portion of the money you make. Investors may also have a say in how you operate your business.

Be sure not to dilute your ownership by taking on too much capital because the more shares you give, the less percentage of the company you own. Also, all money is not good money—you want investors who bring more than money to the table, such as contacts or expertise.

Taking Your Business to Market

Launching and running a business can be challenging. First, you must create a website or identify a space to operate. The most important thing is determining where and how potential customers will find you, your products, or your service.

If you are looking for a website, explore services like Wix, WordPress, and Squarespace, which are some free or low-cost options to help you get started. If you are looking for physical office space, check out Regus and WeWork as options to explore depending on the city you live in for leasing month-to-month office space. However, consider working from home to keep costs down until your business has scaled.

One of the things that are often overlooked but vital to your success is business operations. Business operations are all the activities that help your business run smoothly and productively. You will need to be able to invoice, receive payments, track how your business is performing financially, and communicate with customers to have a successful business.

Square has a good set of payment and invoicing tools that integrate well with other platforms. Intuit has a suite of tools to help you manage your finances, from QuickBooks for accounting purposes to TurboTax for managing your taxes. Another alternative is

FreshBooks, which has affordable invoicing, payments, accounting, and reporting options.

If you are starting an e-commerce business or any other business, Square and Stripe are great payment solutions. They have partnerships with other platforms to make seamless integration into your website or other productivity tools. You can link directly to your business checking account to receive payments for automation.

Sales and Marketing Strategy Basics

To make money, you need to have a steady flow of customers. Therefore, you must create a sales funnel to drive customers to your business. Unfortunately, the adage "if you build it, they will come" is likely not to happen for you. When you first start, customers don't know you exist. So, you need to identify a marketing strategy to drive customers to your business through paid search with Google or advertisements on social media platforms like Instagram and Facebook to connect with potential customers on that platform. A prospective customer needs to hear your message at least seven times before taking action. Therefore, sales and marketing strategies are crucial considerations to ensure you are generating revenue.

It will be important that you learn about customer lifetime value or CLTV. CLTV is the total amount of money a customer is expected to spend on your business or your products during their lifetime. The key component you need to build a strategy around is customer acquisition, as you will need a steady pipeline of customers willing to spend money with you. However, to maximize your revenue, you want to keep those customers regularly spending cash with you—this is called retention. It is often more expensive to acquire new customers, so you must plan to keep your existing customers happy—specifically, the ones who spend the most with you. Often these customers are those who are most engaged with your business. Some helpful books on this topic are *The Customer Centricity Playbook* by Peter Fader and Sarah Toms and *Never Lose a Customer Again* by Joey Coleman.

Branding and Packaging Strategy Basics

Along the same vein as a marketing strategy is your branding and packaging strategy. It would be best if you chose branding and logos that are distinct and professional and communicate the essence of your business to your customers. Once ready for this phase of brand building, you can find a freelancer on Upwork or Fiverr to help you create a simple and distinct logo. I would recommend not going overboard in the beginning until you know you have a sustainable product or service because crap with pretty packaging is still crap, and your customers will quickly figure that out and will not do business with you.

It is a common mistake to overinvest in branding but not invest enough in ensuring you have a fantastic product, excellent customer experience, and unique marketing content customers want to interact with. Spend time researching vendors or asking people in your space of interest which vendors to consider when creating your branded content.

Selecting the wrong vendors can be awfully expensive. For example, let's say you are creating a beauty supply company—branded packaging may be essential to creating an experience for your customers. However, you need to consider the cost of the packaging and how it impacts profits—also, the style, size, and weight of your packaging will impact shipping costs. Most vendors will have pricing that varies based on your purchase volume. However, in the beginning, purchase a small quantity to ensure your packaging choice will work from an operational cost standpoint. Also, you don't want to be out of a lot of money should you determine your business is not viable, or customers don't want your product offering.

Growing Your Business

Now that you have covered some of the fundamentals, I would like to share other tools to consider for growing businesses. As you begin to scale, you may hire employees who need communication and collaboration tools. Many companies will struggle at this stage as the owner needs to figure out how to incorporate others and empower them to help fuel the company's success.

Productivity tools will become important during this stage. Google has a full suite of tools that you can use for email, handling meetings, documents, presentations, and spreadsheets from anywhere. Another great tool is Slack, a robust messaging platform, to cut down emails and back-and-forth communications. If you need to manage projects and tasks, I have used Trello, a dashboard to plan and organize your team's assignments. Other options would be Asana and Basecamp.

Five Business Ideas That Need Little Money

If you are struggling with what business to start or feel it takes a lot of money to start a business, I have included five companies you can start with little to no money. The first business idea is a subscription-based business, which requires a customer to pay a recurring price at regular intervals to access a product. The startup cost for this business is relatively small, as you can leverage several web e-commerce platforms to get started. Next, you will need a product that people want to purchase regularly, such as snacks, toiletries, and other household goods. For example, BarkBox, a subscription service for dog products that started in 2011, provides a monthly delivery of toys, treats, and other essential items for a man's best friend.

The second business idea is a mobile services business, which does not require you to have a fixed location. However, it often requires customers to pay you a premium to come to them for a service that would typically require them to leave their homes; it's all about convenience.

Think about something people would normally leave their homes to take care of frequently. Think of the ones that can be inconvenient. These might be innovative ideas you can use to create your mobile services business. Mobile services business includes companies like mobile carwash services, automobile repair, food trucks, mobile haircare, and cosmetic services—to name a few. Refer to the information about starting a business with an understanding of customer pain points. Then, you must match these pain points to a service you can reasonably provide or outsource effectively. One of my clients, Ogadimma, or Oga, owns a business that perfectly models this concept. Oga is the owner of Pure OG Fitness, a personal training service in Northern California that comes to the homes of busy tech industry clients to help them meet individual fitness goals. He gives clients the convenience of working with a trainer from home, which allows him to provide a premium service. In addition, he makes it easy for the client to book services online and brings all the necessary equipment.

The third business idea is an online training business. Online training is a multibillion-dollar industry and a fantastic way to create another income stream. This type of business involves creating course content based on your expertise that people would benefit from learning.

The first step is to choose a topic. This might be your ideal business if you have the necessary expertise you can turn into a course. Your course should be a topic that aligns with your expertise, passion, and skills.

The next step is identifying the target audience and researching to create a course your audience will value. Several platforms help you make your courses, such as Udemy, Teachable, and Skillshare. One company that provides online training is Wisdify, created by Joe Lucas. It offers online courses to help people improve their analyses and modeling skills to make them competitive in today's business environment. A client can access Wisdify courses on its website and education platforms like Udemy. I recommend testing your content on an audience to get feedback or creating content for free on YouTube before putting it on a paid platform.

A consulting business is the fourth business you can create with very little money. Are people always seeking your expertise to solve a problem? A consulting company may be perfect for you if you have expertise in business, engineering, marketing, or some niche skills others find valuable. For example, Kevin Thibodeaux, a former manager for Accenture, leveraged his knowledge to create Vertist Consultants in 2005, where he successfully provided Change Management consulting services for 16 years before retiring. Clients paid Kevin to solve problems and help the client during crucial transformational initiatives. A consulting firm does require you to trade your time for money, so be sure to take advantage of productivity tools to optimize your time.

At the bare minimum, you will need scheduling software like Calendly, Acuity Scheduling, or Squarespace Scheduling so that clients can book time with you. You will also need to have the ability to accept payments, as I have mentioned in the section about starting a business. Stripe, Square, and PayPal can handle this requirement just fine. You also want a landing page that displays your business name, logo, and services you provide for those interested. Finally, with some marketing, you will be well on your way to starting your new business.

The fifth business you can consider is an editing service. While you probably love writing or can shape a poorly worded document into a masterpiece, many people don't like writing or need help perfecting their documents. Whether working as a freelancer editing different publications, research, or marketing content, a lot of work is available for those who want to start an editing business. Consider signing up on Upwork or Fiverr, two freelancing platforms, to bid for editing work and advertise on professional sites like LinkedIn or social media sites like Facebook or Instagram. For example, Anita, an expert in curriculum development, has successfully leveraged the Upwork platform to secure clients for editing and writing assignments. I recently hired her to help me with some material I needed to create for my coaching business. Freelance editing work is a great way for Anita and many others to earn additional income.

In the next chapter, you will learn about real estate investing and how it can help you achieve financial freedom.

Chapter Summary/Key Takeaways

This chapter focuses on starting your own business. The steps needed to accomplish that goal: finding an idea, developing a business plan, deciding on a legal structure, taking care of administrative tasks, financing the business, designing the branding, marketing the company, and growing the business are critical components in building a solid business that will last.

Also, those worried about not having enough capital to begin a business could start a subscription business, design an online course, establish a mobile service business, or start freelance editing with little to no money.

For these steps to work and for your business to flourish, you must be patient and willing to work hard to make it successful.

Chapter Six
Real Estate Investing Basics

In 2008, I drove three hours from South Carolina to a car dealership in Georgia to purchase a new BMW that I found online through a car-buying service. I remember walking up to this obscure dealership near an industrial park outside Atlanta, Georgia. Preapproval check in my hand, excitement radiated off of me like a beam of sunlight. I was making what I thought was good money and wanted to show the world I had arrived. But, at this time, I wasn't in the wealth mindset. Even though I had bought a Honda Accord three years earlier, which was still driving without issue, I arrogantly thought a BMW would reflect my new status and income level!

I was so excited about the purchase I was ready to make that I called my older brother. "Guess what?" I said. But before he could answer, I told him I was at the dealership buying a brand-new BMW!

Although I expected my brother to be excited about my purchase, I received a rude awakening. Instead, he told me, "Bro, you don't even own a home; how are you going to spend that kind of money on a car that will depreciate as soon as you drive it off the car lot?"

I immediately walked out of the dealership, got back inside my Honda Accord, and drove back to my apartment in South Carolina. Yes, instead of *minding my business* and focusing on building wealth, I was worried about how others would perceive me.

Three months later, I would buy my first home, which has been a great asset for many years. Purchasing a home was the spark I needed to learn more about real estate investing and its associated benefits. This section will give you an overview of real estate investing with helpful tips on why it should be a crucial part of your investment portfolio.

While this is not the definitive guide on real estate investing, I hope to inspire you to learn more about the topic.

Real estate investing is the purchase, ownership, or sale of real estate for a profit. This profit is achieved either through buying a property for a lower amount and selling it for a higher amount after completing construction improvements or when favorable market conditions create a higher valuation. There are several strategies that real estate investors use. They include:

- Buy, fix, and flip
- Buy and hold
- Short-term rentals
- Medium-term rentals

Buy, fix, and flip

The first one is called the buy, fix, and flip strategy. The buy, fix, and flip strategy involves looking for an undervalued property that will appreciate once some cosmetic repairs or remodeling has been completed. My friend Lonnie and his wife are experts in this approach. They have developed a system to find "ugly homes" or homes where the owner cannot maintain the property.

Then, they purchase the property for a value significantly below ARV or after repair value. ARV is the house's value once the home is renovated and sold at market value. They make money on the difference in the house's selling price once the cost of repairing and purchasing the house has been factored in. There are tons of YouTube videos and books on the topic; BiggerPockets has a YouTube channel that offers excellent information on this subject. You need to follow a few basic steps to succeed with the buy, fix, and flip strategy.

Finding the Right Property

Finding the right property is the first step in fixing and flipping a house. You'll want to look for a property that meets the following criteria:

- Proximity to points of interest, like stores, restaurants, and attractions
- Safety of neighborhood
- It requires repairs or renovations
- It's priced below market value
- Close vicinity to places of work and schools
- Good sales activity for homes

To find fix and flip properties, the first place to start is an online search for foreclosure listings or talking to real estate agents in your area. A real estate agent should be able to look up foreclosures listed on the multiple listing service (MLS), which consumers don't have access to. Or you can search online databases like Zillow and Movoto. Then, all you need to do is the following:

- Go to the website, enter your search area, and click "Listing Type."
- Then select "Foreclosures" in the "For Sale" section to view what's available now.
- For what may become available in the future, select "Foreclosed" or "Pre-foreclosure" in the "Potential Listings" section.

Keep in mind that the most profitable opportunity online moves fast.

Next, identify off-market property. You can do this by connecting with real estate wholesalers specializing in buying these properties. You can also identify property that might be an opportunity by driving around neighborhoods or during everyday commutes. Next, you want to look at properties and yards with deferred maintenance. For example, I recently bought a property that was a flip. The lady that originally owned the property had lost her husband and couldn't keep up with the maintenance on such a large property and wanted to move in with one of her daughters.

You can also look for properties that are in foreclosure or tax default. These properties can be found through real estate agents specializing in foreclosures. Other sources for foreclosures are government agencies, including Fannie Mae, the Federal Housing Administration, the Treasury Department, and Small Business Administration. Another source is public records. It's free, and you may find newly posted properties that haven't yet reached many online foreclosure data providers.

As part of the foreclosure process, various legal notices must be filed in your county recorder's office. This information is public record and available to anyone. Just visit your county's office, and you can search for a Notice of Default (NOD), lis pendens, or Notice of Sale. Once you've found a few potential properties, it's time to determine their economic value. In other words, can you make money?

Estimate Repair Cost

The next step is to estimate the repair costs. This is important because you need to know how much money you'll need to finance the purchase and renovation of the property. Talk to contractors or look at online cost estimators to get an accurate estimate. Be sure to include a contingency fund in your estimate to cover unexpected repairs. One of the rules I learned from my mentor and friend Lonnie is the 65% rule. This guideline says you should buy the property for 65% of its after-repair value minus the rehab costs.

For example, if a property is worth $100K and needs $20K in rehab, you should buy this particular property for 65% of $100K = $65K - $20K (rehab) = $45K. This rule is in place because you could lose up to 10% in closing expenses during purchase and sale. You want a 5% buffer for the unexpected. Finally, most flippers would like to make a 20% profit on the deal.

The bottom line is that when you're flipping property, your profit margin is the key to success. The less profit margin you have, not only is your profit potential lower, but your risk is also higher. To truly succeed, you need all the margin you can get.

Buy and Hold

The second one is called the buy-and-hold strategy. The buy-and-hold strategy is the one using the property as an additional stream of income and falls under the multiple income streams strategy. This strategy requires you to lease the property to a renter for more than the mortgage payment due on the property. Rental income from the property generates short-term income that can be used to pay off the mortgage and put cash in the investor's wallet.

In addition, the property value will appreciate over time, allowing investors to profit when they are ready to sell the property down the line. As a result, you make income by leveraging the renter to pay all the fees associated with financing the house. At the same time, you benefit from the equity buildup and any remaining cash flow after expenses.

Finding the Right Property

A good buy-and-hold property starts with finding the right property. Finding a property for long-term investing can be similar to finding one to fix and flip. Some criteria to consider are as follows:

- Proximity to points of interest, like stores, restaurants, and attractions
- Safety of neighborhood
- Quality of the schools zoned for the home
- Average growth in home prices
- Average rental rates
- Income and employment statistics
- County and community zoning and restrictions

Location will be a pivotal part of your buy-and-hold strategy's success. Your location will directly impact how much you can charge tenants for rent, how much property value will appreciate, and the overall value. For example, it will be difficult to charge higher rents if you buy property in a place with high crime, poor-performing schools, and lower incomes. Conversely, some investors will identify areas like this that are near growth areas and may be transitioning to a middle- or upper-class neighborhood to purchase the property in anticipation of the area improving in property value over time.

They will typically pay lower prices to buy these homes, bring them up to standard with renovations, and later charge higher rents or benefit from the appreciation once the yoga studios and fancy coffee shops start popping up. When looking for rentals, I typically look for areas with population growth, multiple industries, and a large working-class population.

This works especially well for multifamily properties. Multifamily properties are properties containing two or more units in a single dwelling. In addition, when looking at specific properties, I look for areas with a decent commute to the major employers, low crime rates, proximity to grocery stores, quality schools, parks, and access to highways and public transportation.

Similar to fix and flip, you can leverage real estate agents, online sources, government websites, and public records to find a property. If it is a market you are not as familiar with, a good realtor will provide you with valuable information about it. However, I would advise you to research, as realtors can be biased and incentivized to direct you to certain areas.

Evaluating Properties

When purchasing a home to own and occupy, you want to look at comparable home sales, which means establishing how much similar homes are selling for in an area to determine if the price is reasonable. At the same time, this is still important for an investor. The mindset for purchasing real estate investments has to be approached like running a business. This means the property has to cash flow or make enough rental income to cover expenses. I don't make a purchase decision on the potential for the property to appreciate in value alone!

This means that you want to understand relative rent income to value and ensure you will get a return on investment; you don't want to pay so much for a property that the amount of rent you need to charge to break even is more than anyone is willing to pay. At a minimum, the rent should cover your mortgage payment on the property. Another commonly used approach is the **1% rule**. This rule states that you should get at least 1% of the property's purchase price in monthly rent.

However, I generally go by 2% since this may not be feasible in some markets. Ideally, you want to find a property that can attract market or above-market rents. This means that your property is up to standard for the area, has the right amenities, and is located in a great neighborhood.

The goal should be to get a property that will allow you to get the highest possible rent with minor changes. Additionally, you want to find a house in an area that is ideal for renters with good rental rates that will increase over time. Several websites like Rentometer and RentCafe can help you determine rental rates.

You also want to be in a place with high rental occupancy and long-term renters. Since you may want to sell it at a much later date, in 15 to 20 years, you should understand whether the property is positioned to appreciate in value over time. Find out what plans the city has for this area. Is it an area that will be invested in over time? Are retailers and employers considering a building or establishing a presence in that area? Are employment and population statistics like income, population growth, and employment improving in the area?

As I mentioned, you must have a business mindset when investing in real estate. This means understanding the metrics professional real estate investors use.

One easy financial measure to estimate is *net income*—you can calculate this by subtracting expenses like taxes, maintenance, HOA fees, and property management fees from the average rent you believe you can get for the property. If it's negative, it probably will not be a worthwhile investment. I also look at *annual cash flow*, which takes the net income and subtracts the mortgage payment.

In some cases, it is ok to have low yearly cash flow in the first year if you believe the property will appreciate, or you can increase the rent quickly to increase the annual cash flow.

Another term to understand is *capitalization rate*—cap rate for short—which is the rate of return expected from the property. It is often used as a comparison tool between similar properties. The cap rate is calculated by dividing the net income by the property's purchase price to get a percentage. A good realtor can tell you typical cap rates for a location. Generally, eight percent or better is good, but it depends on the market.

It is also important to warn against using this measure alone to select a property. However, it would be best to calculate an approximate cap rate to get an idea of the return rate. For example, you divide the property's purchase price by the annual rental payment. This calculation is helpful to decide if you want to look at the property or whether to make a lower offer to get the rate of return you desire.

For example, if a property is for sale for $200,000 and you can get $30,000 in rent yearly, that is approximately a return rate of 15%. Remember that this doesn't consider all the costs but gives you a quick way to compare two similar properties.

Another measure is *cash-on-cash return*, which looks at how much you invest in the property with your own money relative to the cash flow from purchasing the property. Cash-on-cash return is calculated by dividing the annual cash flow from the property by the down payment.

For example, if you put $40,000 cash into a property with a net annual cash flow of $10,000 a year, your return rate would be 25%. So essentially, you are getting a 25% return on your investment from your cash.

These calculations are not an exhaustive list but give you a few tools to help evaluate properties as you increase your knowledge. It would be best if you don't use any of these measures in isolation to decide because they are more powerful together.

The critical point is to make sure you are not losing money on an investment to build for your future.

I will also note that many successful investors have made income streams with varied investment strategies. Some people have done well by buying lots of lower-priced homes in rural communities, essentially becoming big fish in a small pond. Others have done well focusing on low-income dwellings that the government subsidizes. If real estate investing is for you, spend time developing your own strategy.

Managing Investment Properties

You will pay the mortgage, taxes, and insurance as a landlord. You will also be required to find a tenant and deal with issues such as necessary maintenance or repairs. Based on my experience, you should consider hiring a property management company to handle tenant issues to help make the asset as reasonably passive as possible.

Property management companies usually ask for five to ten percent of the rent collected, depending on the location and number of properties they are managing for you. Question property management fees beyond ten percent because this is a potential red flag. You must do your due diligence to evaluate the quality of the property management service by asking questions about their experience in managing properties and checking out any reviews for them online through platforms such as Yelp or the Better Business Bureau (BBB).

I had to let go of the first property management company I hired because they misappropriated funds. I would not have made this mistake if I had looked at reviews indicating their poor services. The following company I hired worked well and continues to manage my property. However, this was a painful lesson to learn.

If you choose to self-manage the property, there are many digital tools on the market to make this less hassle. Tools like Cozy, an online tool to collect and manage rent payments, might be right for you. Also, check out Zillow, as it now has tools to help you manage and market your rental property.

Short-Term Rentals

Another buy-and-hold strategy is to use the property for short-term rentals. Short-term rental refers to a fully furnished residential unit—either the entire house, a room, or any living space in the home—that owners rent out to guests for a short period.

In general, short-term rentals are rented out for less than 30 days. They are considered an alternative to a hotel. Sometimes, short-term rentals are referred to as vacation, Airbnb, transient, and home-sharing. Often, you can find them listed on home-sharing platforms like Airbnb, VRBO, and Travel Nursing.

After a decade of profiting off a long-term buy-and-hold strategy, I started leveraging the short-term rental strategy a few years ago.

I purchased a property with a mother-in-law suite. The mother-in-law suite, located on the basement level, has its own entrance and kitchen. The strategy was to live in a part of the home and rent out the basement to guests on platforms like Airbnb. This home was particularly appealing because of its proximity to the Six Flags Amusement Park, Brave's Baseball Stadium, and other attractions. From a purchasing standpoint, purchasing property for short-term rental is similar to other buy-and-hold properties. We will cover some additional considerations.

Finding the Right Property

When identifying the right property, there are a few things you should consider:

- Demand for vacation rentals
- Proximity to tourist attractions
- Cost of housing
- Short-term rental rules and restrictions
- Performance of similar rentals

The best short-term rental markets are those that are close to tourist attractions. The major source of business for short-term rentals is tourists and leisure travelers. Therefore, choosing a place strategically located near tourist spots will increase its chance of getting a high occupancy rate. Other areas to consider are those near military installations, universities, and major hospitals. For example, I once stayed at an Airbnb where the owner's strategy was to provide housing for nurses and families visiting St. Jude Children's Research Hospital in Memphis, Tennessee.

Cost is an important factor when getting into short-term rentals. If you want to become a successful investor, you don't want to choose a real estate market with expensive housing. The best place to buy a short-term rental property is one that is considered affordable—it allows you to earn a better return on investment. I think older homes can make great short-term rentals because of the cost. Make sure also to choose a market with a steady appreciation rate.

Also, remember that these types of rentals are furnished. So make a budget for furnishing the home and stick to that budget. At the same time, if you want to differentiate and have a nice-looking home, make sure not to overspend.

Make sure to choose a location where it is legal to operate a short-term rental business. You need to check your city's short-term rental rules and regulations to do it. Moreover, you also need to know the restrictions related to operating a short-term rental property. In some cities, local ordinances allow short-term rentals as long as they comply with the restrictions.

For instance, in some markets, vacation rentals are considered legal if they are owner-occupied. However, it means that the owner needs to be present at home with the guests. In addition to state laws and city ordinances, you must also ensure that short-term rentals are allowed in the village or condominium where the property is located. If you're planning to buy a property in a village or a condominium complex, check the homeowners' association or condominium agreement. Doing so will ensure that you won't encounter any issues later on.

Evaluating Short-Term Properties

The next thing to understand is the local market for short-term rentals. Again, you can leverage platforms like AirDNA to get data on various short-term rental markets with Airbnb properties.

Here are a few data points you want to review before using a property for short-term rentals:

- Occupancy rate is the number of days a guest rents a property during a specific period (If you rent your property for 21 days out of a 30-day month, 21/30 = 70%).
- The average daily rate (ADR) is the daily revenue that a room can earn.
- The average length of stay (ALOS) represents the average number of nights booked by a guest.
- Revenue per available room (RevPAR) is the amount of money made per available room (RevPAR = average daily rate x occupancy rate).
- Cap rate is considered an essential metric to determine a property's profitability. It is the rate of return based on the property's purchase price or current market value.
- Cash-on-cash return refers to the rate of return based on your initial cash investment in the property.

- The method of financing you choose and the amount of your down payment will significantly affect the cash-on-cash return value.
- Cash flow refers to the amount of cash you can generate from your investment property. A positive cash flow shows that the property generates a profit after deducting the expenses. On the other hand, a negative cash flow indicates that the property doesn't generate enough income to cover the costs of owning a rental.

The bottom line is that short-term rentals can be an excellent investment strategy for any serious real estate investor. With the right property, rental strategy, and investment tools, it can yield generous returns.

Medium-Term Rentals

Most buy-and-hold investors and property owners only think about the two traditional ways to rent a property, long term and short term, but the demand for medium-term rentals is booming!

Below are some reasons:

- A huge increase in remote workers
- Cities are limiting or prohibiting short-term rentals
- Economic shifts create more budget vacationers and, therefore, lower short-term bookings

So, what are medium-term rentals? Medium-term rentals (MTR) are fully furnished properties with utilities designated for remote workers, relocating families staying for 30+ days at a time, temporary corporate assignments, and families looking for temporary stays due to insurance claims or home repairs. Recognizing that the short-term rental market is changing, the medium-term rental investment strategy is now a stand-alone category for real estate investors.

These tenants stay for an average of three or four months; often, the length of stay alone will protect you from your local short-term rental regulations.

Incorporate Medium-Term Rentals into Your Buy-and-Hold Strategy

First, set monthly rates on traditional short-term booking platforms like Airbnb. Airbnb can set monthly rates instead of daily ones, allowing you to give guests a discount on more extended stays. This approach requires a pricing strategy called length-of-stay (LOS) pricing. The longer a guest is looking to stay, the bigger the discount they will get. You can set this up directly in your Airbnb account. Guests looking to book longer stays actively search for properties that have a monthly rate.

Next, get listed on niche websites specializing in medium-term rentals.

Here are five niche booking sites specialized in medium-term rentals we recommend you get listed on as soon as you can:

- HouseStay
- MagicStay
- Landing
- Mint House
- Blueground

Lastly, optimize your rental for medium-term bookings. Think about the type of guest you're trying to attract and adapt your rentals' amenities to their needs. Guests staying for 30 days or longer are not tourists. They are most likely people in between places living their day-to-day lives. They will most likely be setting up their home office in your rental. To attract these types of guests, it's a good idea to equip your rental with all the amenities they may need. Once you've done that, update your listings and upload new photographs showcasing how your rental can be turned into a temporary home/workspace.

Make sure that your rental has the following:

- A fully equipped kitchen
- A coffee machine
- A comfortable desk or other workspaces
- High-speed internet

Real Estate Financing

Now that you are familiar with some of the various real estate strategies, it's time to talk about financing properties. When buying real estate, you want to use as much of other people's money as possible, which usually means financing with a bank or investors. Therefore, securing funding is one of the first steps in buying a property. Consequently, it is crucial to have your financing sorted out before you start looking at properties.

If you think you will need financing, one of the first places to go is the bank to lock down financing. Good credit is a significant factor in your ability to secure a loan.

You do not need a perfect score of 850 to get a reasonable interest rate. Generally, you can qualify for a loan with a credit score of 650, but scores around 740 will give you the best rate for a loan. The bank will also want to see financial statements to assess the risk of lending you money, so be prepared to provide updated financial information.

Criteria for securing a loan vary depending on the financial institution, so shop around and consult various banks. Generally, banks will only finance a loan-to-value (LTV) of 75–90% of the property's value, so you need to be prepared with anywhere from a 10–25% down payment of your own money or an investor. In addition, there are several financing options available to you, depending on your situation.

The loan type that most people will use to buy a home is a *conventional loan*. Conventional loans are home loans without any direct government backing. This loan type generally has an LTV of

80–95% with interest rates determined by the market, and payment terms are usually 10, 15, 20, and 30 years.

Loans can either be conforming or nonconforming loans. Conforming loans have to meet standards determined by the two quasi-government entities, Fannie Mae and Freddie Mac. Nonconforming loans are used by individuals who want to buy homes that exceed those limits.

The loan is secured on the borrower's property through a process known as mortgage origination. If you don't pay, the bank has the legal right to take your home and put your stuff on the side of the road—yikes!

Another commonly used type of home loan is *a government-backed loan*. These loans include loans guaranteed by government agencies such as the Federal Housing Authority (FHA) and the Department of Veteran Affairs (VA). These organizations have programs geared toward first-time buyers who plan to live in the home. One strategy you can use is to use one of these programs to purchase a home for little to no money down, live in the property for a while, then make it a rental home after you buy the next house. I employed this strategy and purchased my first home and subsequent rental property.

The third loan type is *private lending*, where a home loan is financed through a private source of funds, such as friends, family, or a business, rather than a traditional mortgage lender.

Private lending is an excellent option if bank financing is unavailable and could lead to more favorable interest rates and terms. While this type of loan can benefit all parties involved, this method has several risks if not structured correctly. I suggest creating a formal agreement and consulting an attorney if you decide to go this route.

The fourth type of loan is called *hard money lending*. Hard money loans are primarily used for real estate transactions, and the money comes from an individual or company, not a bank. These loans are taken out for a short time and can be a quicker way to secure funds for a property purchase. These loans typically have a very high cost, a lower LTV ratio (70% or less), and terms of one to three years. They are generally used by individuals who plan to renovate a property and sell it quickly.

Another type of financing is called *seller financing*. Seller financing is a creative way to purchase a property by striking an agreement with the seller rather than a bank loan.

Essentially, the purchaser will make a down payment to the seller and then make installments over a specified time at an agreed-upon interest rate until the loan is fully repaid.

A lesser-known method for financing real estate is via a *self-directed individual retirement* account (IRA). A self-directed IRA is, at its most basic level, a savings account that allows for compounded, tax-free growth over time. Self-directed IRAs are unique from other savings accounts, such as a 401(k), as the owner can control various investment options, including real estate. In addition, owners of self-directed IRA accounts enjoy the unique benefit of purchasing, rehabbing, and selling properties while still being able to defer taxes. However, it is important to note that owners under 60 years of age are typically subject to a penalty for withdrawing funds early.

Real Estate Groups & Syndication Deals

When most people think of investing in real estate, they think about buying a single-family home, renting it out, and collecting monthly rent checks. However, another consideration is to invest as a collective.

I have done this twice, domestically and internationally, with a real estate group investment known as *real estate syndication*. Through real estate syndication, you invest your money in real estate with a group of other passive investors in a limited partnership. However, you don't have to do any day-to-day work managing the property and collecting steady cash flow. After establishing an investment chat group, a few of my fraternity brothers and I decided to pool our resources and raise $100K to invest in real estate. We created an LLC with an operating agreement and opened a bank account. We listened to investment pitches for several real estate projects within a week. Ultimately, we invested in a 16-unit apartment complex for student housing in South Carolina. This investment gives us quarterly dividends based on the profitability of the property.

Before you jump into a real estate investment group, here are a few things you should consider:

- Minimum investment amounts
- Projected returns
- Understanding your liquidity and ability to invest
- Agreements
- Taxes

Minimum Investment Amount

The minimum real estate investment for each different real estate syndication can vary. The minimum investment I have seen is $50,000. This means you can invest $50,000 or more into a real estate syndicate in increments of $5,000. So when my business partners Jermaine and Richard reached out to me about an opportunity to purchase a 7-bedroom, 7.5-bathroom villa in Tulum, Mexico, I was excited. The real estate market in the U.S. was difficult. Properties were overvalued, and we lost every bid to corporate investors with deep pockets.

So we created a real estate investment group by establishing a corporate entity and identified members who added value to the group. Each member contributed $56,500 for a percentage of ownership.

We took ownership of the property, added our personal touches to the design, and listed it for short-term rentals. So far, this property is cash-flowing.

Projected Returns

And what about the returns? How much money could you stand to make through investing in a real estate syndication? The answer is that it depends on the individual syndication and its structure. But let's look at an example of a real estate syndicate to give you a general benchmark for what to expect.

For example, let's say you invested in an apartment real estate syndication with a projected five-year hold. Let's say that real estate investors each put $100,000 into this syndication. A projected annual return of 8% means that real estate investors in commercial properties could expect to get 8% of their original investment per year.

Over the five-year hold period, this comes out to $40,000 in returns. And then, there's the profit from the sale of the property in year five. Let's say the property sells for what you paid for it.

In most cases, the property would appreciate in value. However, I'm being conservative. In other words, by the end of the real estate syndication, you would have gotten your $100,000 original investment back—$40,000 in returns during those five years.

Understanding Your Liquidity & Ability to Invest

Because this is a long-term investing strategy, you should only invest in a real estate syndication with money you won't need for several years. Also, if you only have $50,000 in your bank account, please don't invest all of it into commercial real estate syndication as a passive investor. Instead, it would be best to focus on ensuring you have an emergency fund, adequate savings, and other more liquid investments before investing in a long-term project like real estate syndication.

Agreements & Legal Documents

Suppose you decide to invest with a group or through real estate syndication. Make sure you have an operating agreement with the syndication.

In fact, in a real estate deal where you invest your money, you should have at least a promissory note listing you as someone who should be compensated in the event of a transaction. Please consult an attorney before signing any agreements. However, for the operating agreement, the following are some of the sections that should be covered:

- Formation details: What is the name of the LLC, the address, the purpose of the LLC (which relates to the articles that were filed previously), whom to notify, and where books and records are kept.
- Members: Be able to identify what a member is, and then identify what different classes there are if there are other classes.
- Voting rights: What is the voting process, and what voting rights do members have?
- Manager compensation: Be able to identify all fees and where and how to get them paid.
- Capital contributions: How is it that you receive money? Does it go into a specific account? Initial capital contributions? How do you make any additional capital contributions that are needed? What happens when there is that need?
- Dissolution of the agreement: How the deal is terminated and the subsequent process to distribute funds or assets.
- Right of first refusal: This will determine whether you will have first right on the sale of shares.

Real Estate Group Investing Taxes

Another important thing to know is that because you're investing in an LLC, a pass-through entity, you get all of the tax benefits associated with real estate investing. So I recommend you talk to your CPA to learn more about the tax benefits of investing in real estate syndications.

Exit Strategies

Whatever investment strategy you choose, it is crucial to have an end goal in mind. Determine how you will maximize your investments and grow your portfolio over time. One of the primary ways real estate investors use the buy-and-hold strategy to make money is from the gains realized from the appreciation of the property value upon sale. When the property appreciates, you can use the profit from the sale to invest in other assets, fund your freedom, or invest in additional properties. You can also take the cash value associated with the appreciation as a down payment for a different property by refinancing and taking the difference between what you owe and the property's value. For example, if your property value is appraised at $200,0000 and you owe $150,000, you can take some of the difference to reinvest in a second property.

I caution you that real estate values fluctuate or decline despite the widespread belief that prices always increase. Therefore, I rarely decide on a property based on the potential of the property to appreciate alone. The ability for the property to cash flow from renters and other reoccurring revenue will always be the least risky proposition.

Additionally, many investors will start with single-family homes or two to four units as those are usually easier to finance. As you get into more units, it becomes commercial real estate finance, which is more difficult to get bank financing. This real estate strategy means developing a history of stable rental income from a single property or property portfolio and using that history of successfully operating to go to the bank to secure a loan to purchase a property with more units—essentially expanding your empire.

There are many such strategies that investors use to grow. With research, mentorship, and practical experience, you can develop a personalized approach based on your goals, resources, and risk profile.

BiggerPockets, an online community that discusses everything about real estate investing, is a great place to learn more about real estate investment. You can also read influential books such as *Building Wealth One House at a Time* by John Schaub and *What Every Real Estate Investor Needs to Know about Cash Flow* by Frank Gallinelli. The next chapter will teach you about security investments to make your money work.

Chapter Summary/Key Takeaways

Investing in real estate can be highly profitable and equally risky. Therefore, researching areas you are interested in purchasing real estate is paramount in making a sound investment. Using strategies such as buy and hold or buy, fix, and flip will help you make the most out of your real estate purchase. In addition, research the different types of financing to make the most out of your money without getting into deep financial trouble. Purchasing real estate can yield some long-term dividends but researching what you want and need to be successful in this venture is extremely important, and you cannot cut corners while completing this task. Finally, consider talking to realtors about unfamiliar areas to ensure you will not purchase a property with high crime rates or a lack of quality schools. Real estate can be a great way to beef up your financial portfolio but understand that it will take hard work and a lot of research to succeed.

Chapter Seven
Securities Investing (Stocks, Bonds, etc.)

As I mentioned before, I grew up poor near the Mississippi River Delta. I witnessed a lot of poverty and saw the look of despair in so many struggling families that felt stuck in a perpetual cycle of hard work but never seemed to get ahead financially. Experiencing this type of despair made me very adamant about learning everything about investing and wealth creation. But, similar to many Americans, I wasn't taught financial literacy, nor did I know anything about investing in the financial markets. I knew that financial literacy wasn't being taught in school, and it seemed like the people who knew the secret to financial success held on to it like a map to the proverbial buried pirate treasure.

I started my journey learning about investing in stocks in 2006 after reading books on investing, like *The Intelligent Investor* by Benjamin Graham. My first investment experience was while serving in the U.S. Air Force, where I started putting cash in the market while deployed to Afghanistan. One of the senior enlisted members of my team was enthusiastic about trading stocks and encouraged me to get started on investing. Our conversations sparked a fire inside me that inspired me to take investing much more seriously.

Anyone who has ever deployed with the military will tell you that one of the things you look forward to getting is a care package with snacks, entertainment, and other items from home. I was so engulfed in my pursuit of obtaining knowledge about investing that anytime someone wanted to send me a care package, I asked them to include books on investing. I have been hooked on investing ever since!

This section will give you an overview of different securities to equip you with fundamental knowledge on the subject and perhaps inspire you to invest in the market. Let's begin by defining the term *security*, an umbrella term encompassing a broader group of financial assets leveraged in open financial markets. Investopedia defines security as a "fungible, negotiable financial instrument that holds some type of monetary value." It represents an ownership position in a publicly-traded corporation via stock, a creditor relationship with a governmental body or a corporation represented by owning that entity's bond, or rights to ownership as represented by an option.

There are two main securities classes: *equity securities* and *debt securities*. First, let's examine debt securities since much focus will be on stock. Debt is usually issued in the form of a bond. A bond is borrowed money that must be repaid, with terms that stipulate the size of the loan, interest rate, date when full payment is due, or options for renewal. Debt owners make money by being paid a principal amount plus interest. Debt investments differ from equity because returns are predetermined based on interest rates. As a result, returns are generally less predictable and have a definitive end date, and debt owners are usually paid first in bankruptcy.

On the other hand, equity securities such as stocks are fractional ownership of a particular company. Unlike debt securities such as bonds, equity securities do not guarantee a monthly payment—although some stocks provide a payment to owners called a dividend. Instead, the returns occur when the stock appreciates due to the company's positive performance and other market conditions that cause the stock price to increase. This appreciation in stock value is called a *capital gain*, which you can either take immediately by selling the stock or holding the stock over time to realize long-term growth.

The wealthy favor income from stock because it is taxed much lower than earned income. Stock trading requires patience and should not be done with a gambler's mentality. In fact, buying and holding is a strategy that many investors deploy for portions of their portfolios. The buy-and-hold strategy does not mean you should not monitor and pay attention to the market. The stock market will fluctuate up and down in value, which is known as market volatility, but the market yields a net positive over the long run.

According to Goldman Sachs, the average stock market return for ten years has been about nine percent (2021). For example, I bought shares of Apple for $99 per share around 2015. However, around 2020, the stock reached a value of approximately $400 per share before the company announced a 4-for-1 stock split. A share split means that for every stock you own, the company gives you additional shares, which equals the value of the original share.

One of the fundamental concepts you must understand about investing in stocks is the notion of risk versus reward. Since stocks are inherently risky, you must have a strategy to maximize return and mitigate losses. One way to mitigate risk is to diversify your portfolio with stocks in different industries, sectors, and companies. Risk mitigation follows the adage: don't put all of your eggs in one basket. A diversified portfolio reduces investment risk from market fluctuations in a specific company, sector, or industry and spreads the risk across the board. As a result, if one investment fails, the performance of other investments attempts to balance the risk.

Following stock market trends is one of the risk management strategies which helps you to decide whether you should invest or not. Following stock market trends involves looking at stock charts, such as a candlestick chart, to determine when to buy or sell based on whether the market is trending up or down. A candlestick chart is a price chart that shows a security's high, low, and open-closing prices during a specific period. Traders commonly use candlestick charts to predict price movements using past pricing patterns.

Having a strategy that aligns with your risk-taking tolerance and doesn't put all your money at risk in one trade is necessary. You must also plan your trades by determining an open and close position aligned to a specific exit. Since stocks fluctuate up and down, you should know the lowest point you are willing to let the stock price fall to prevent further loss—this action is called a *stop loss*, and it helps you minimize your losses from downward stock movement.

On the upside, you must determine the target price you are willing to sell your stock to book profits—we call this *taking profits*. It's important to book profits as stocks will eventually reach a resistance level and decrease after that. An effective trading strategy requires understanding the risk-reward ratio. The risk-reward ratio measures the potential profit for every dollar risked. It is the ratio between potential profit and the amount at risk. For example, if you buy a stock for $20 with a profit target of $22 and set a stop-loss of $19 as the lowest value you are willing to risk before exiting the position, the risk-reward ratio is 1:2 because you're risking one dollar to make two dollars.

Now that we have an overview of securities, let's look at security investing from an overall portfolio view. An investment portfolio is like a treasure chest of financial assets containing stocks, bonds, cash, and more. Investors seek returns by blending these securities based on individual risk tolerance and short- and long-term financial objectives.

Diversifying with a blended portfolio of assets is another way of managing risk. This approach of creating an investment portfolio and thoughtful planning on how different financial asset classes will mix together within the portfolio is known as an *asset allocation strategy*. Asset allocation is an investment technique that balances risk with a portfolio by distributing assets across broad investment classes such as cash, bonds, stocks, real estate, and other investment types.

Asset allocation is beneficial because each asset class has different return and risk levels and will behave differently over time. For example, bonds have lower returns but low risk. Conversely, stocks have high risks but high rewards.

Several allocation strategies have been leveraged over time. One rule of thumb that has helped simplify asset allocation states that individuals should hold a percentage of stocks equal to 100 minus their age. The rest would comprise high-grade bonds, government debt, and other relatively safe assets.

However, following a person's age is probably not as useful today since we have experienced significant changes in the bond markets that have caused experts to rethink this long-time philosophy. Generally, bond yields tend to go up as interest rates fall—the opposite is also true. After three decades of downward movement, interest rates have slowly increased from all-time lows.

Another important factor is that people live much longer and pay for a longer retirement in a shorter period, which means you need to realize more gains from stocks. Therefore, another rule called the 15/50 stock rule may be more relevant. This rule says that if you believe you have more than 15 years left, your portfolio should consist of at least 50% stocks, with the remaining balance in bonds, cash, and other investments. This approach helps you maintain a balance between risk and reward. Whenever possible, you must research and consult relevant investing, tax, and estate planning experts to ensure you have the most up-to-date information to create the best portfolio for your unique situation.

The allocation of stocks versus other assets in a portfolio is essential in a portfolio allocation strategy. When you invest in a stock, you purchase fractional ownership of that company. Therefore, putting all your money into one stock is never good. This principle also includes stock in the company you work for unless that stock is in the form of compensation and doesn't require trading in cash for ownership. Investing in many stocks across various industries is better for spreading the risk.

Many experts believe that stock diversification isn't fully realized until your portfolio holds around 20 stocks from companies operating in different industries and sectors. Once you own 20 or more stocks, the remaining risk is considered a market-wide risk, the average risk everyone endures, versus idiosyncratic risk, which refers to the risk inherent to that specific security.

One instrument that helps you diversify is a *mutual fund*, which offers more diversification by bundling many company stocks into one investment. Mutual funds are great because the fund manager does the diversification for you. Another benefit of mutual funds is that investors can put a small amount of money into one or more funds and access a diverse pool of investment options, unlike stocks. Therefore, you can buy a unit of a mutual fund that invests in dozens of different securities. On the other hand, it would require substantially more cash to get the same diversification and results in the stock market by purchasing individual stock.

Another asset type to be aware of is an *index fund*, which is often confused with a mutual fund. The main difference between index funds and mutual funds is that index funds invest in a specific set of securities, such as only stocks traded on the S&P 500 or the New York Stock Exchange.

In contrast, an investment fund manager chooses mutual funds. Index funds are designed to follow the market average, while actively managed mutual funds attempt to beat the market performance. The result is that index fund performance is relatively predictable over long periods and mutual funds have more variability in performance. In addition, the expense is higher due to the involvement of investment fund managers in managing mutual funds.

An alternative asset type to consider is an *exchange-traded fund* (ETF). An ETF is similar to a mutual fund in that it diversifies and reduces risk but differs from a mutual fund because it can trade throughout the day just like an individual stock, as opposed to only trading at the end of the day like a traditional mutual fund. Additionally, passively managed ETFs generally have lower expense ratios than actively managed mutual funds.

Investing in ETFs gives you the benefits of mutual funds without the added cost of active management and the liquidity and flexibility that comes with investing in individual stocks.

For that reason, I have personally increased my investment in ETFs over the years. For example, I was investing in individual cannabis stocks to varying degrees of success before focusing on ETFs investing in the cannabis space.

On the other hand, it is important to note that ETFs aren't designed to beat the market but to follow a particular market index. When the underlying index rises or falls, the ETF eventually follows. Depending on your investment strategy, index funds and ETFs can be attractive over actively managed mutual funds because of the lower expense and because actively managed funds rarely beat the market. I am a huge proponent of mutual funds, index funds, and ETFs, which is why most of the stocks in my portfolio are mutual funds and ETFs. Right now, only about 20–25% of the stock portion of my portfolio consists of individual stocks.

In the next chapter, you will learn about alternative investments you can add to your portfolio.

Chapter Summary/Key Takeaways

This chapter focuses on the various types of security investments you can make to increase your financial portfolio. There are two main types of security investments: equity and debt securities.

In addition, you have stocks, bonds, EFTs, mutual funds, and index funds within those types.

Each of these investments has varying levels of risks and returns and can help you grow your nest egg for retirement.

Also, having a strategy for asset allocation or portfolio allocation will allow you to maximize your profitability and mitigate some risks.

Finally, you must decide how much cash you are willing to risk and understand its impact on your finances, whether you gain or lose big in the stock market.

Chapter Eight
Introduction To Alternative Investments

Finally, we will discuss alternative market-based investments outside traditional securities like rare metals, currencies, commodities, cryptocurrencies, and cash-value insurance. According to the Chartered Alternative Investment Analyst Association, or CAIA, interest in alternative investments is growing from 6% to 12% of the global market, with an 18–24% increase by 2025 (2019). I believe we will see alternative investments become increasingly mainstream options for portfolio diversification over time. The growth is mainly fueled by high-net-worth individuals and institutional investors looking for increased portfolio returns.

With that said, alternative investments are not for every investor. Access is limited to high-net-worth individuals and entities who can invest in securities that are not always disclosed to financial regulators.

These investors are categorized into two groups: *accredited investors* and *qualified purchasers*. Accredited investors must have an individual income exceeding $200,000—or $300,000 for joint income—for the last two years and expect their earnings to continue at that threshold or have an individual or collective net worth exceeding one million dollars. Qualified investors have an investment portfolio of five million dollars or more, individually or jointly. These people are considered experienced investors or have access to advanced information or advisors; however, more and more of these opportunities are opening up for the average investor. In October 2021, the U.S. Securities and Exchange Commission expanded those definitions to include specific educational requirements for people in the finance industry.

Currency Investing

The currency market is one of the oldest financial markets to exist. The first Foreign Exchange Market ("Forex") began in Amsterdam nearly 500 years ago. Established in the 1970s, the modern-day market is the largest, critical to global commerce, and determines foreign exchange rates for every country. The major player in the foreign exchange market is international banks. This market represents the largest asset class globally, with a huge volume of trading 24 hours daily except for weekends and nearly seven trillion dollars of activity daily. Investing in currency involves buying one country's currency while selling that of another. Forex trading always happens in pairs; for a transaction to be complete, one currency has to be exchanged for another. So, for example, you might buy U.S. dollars (USD) and sell British pounds (GBP)—or vice versa. While you could technically exchange any foreign currency traded on the market exchange for another, it's more common to trade using pre-established pairings.

The premise of Forex trading is that you make money by capitalizing on the fluctuations in currency value. Like trading stocks, you want the currency you buy to increase in value so you can sell it at a profit. Therefore, your profit is attached to the currency's exchange rate, the ratio of one currency's value against another. However, stocks and mutual funds differ from Forex because they are traded on a centralized exchange such as the Nasdaq or New York Stock Exchange (NYSE). Forex is decentralized with interconnected marketplaces where different currency instruments are traded. In the foreign exchange market, banks and other financial institutions in London, New York, and Hong Kong drive most of the activity.

As mentioned earlier, it is the largest financial market globally, but one in which many individual investors have never attempted to trade because it's highly speculative and complex. Similar to securities, like stock, Forex trading is through a brokerage—these can be the same brokerage used for stock trading or brokerages specializing in Forex.

There are two main ways you can trade foreign currency. First, *spread betting* allows you to speculate on the price movement of a pair of currencies without buying or selling them. *Spot Forex trading* necessitates traders to buy and sell currency pairs at the current market price, also known as the spot price. Like stock trading, each enables you to go long and short on currency pairs working slightly differently.

Spot Forex trading is when you buy and sell currencies. Here's how it works: currencies are always traded in pairs, such as the EUR and the USD. When you trade Forex, you always buy one currency and sell another. For example, the EUR may rise while the USD falls based on geopolitical or economic factors like natural disasters or elections. Based on those factors, you might then buy EUR and sell USD. If your prediction pans out and the EUR does rise in value, you will make a profit. It is important to remember that you're always buying or selling the base currency. One currency will always be the base within a pair, and one will always be the counter.

The EUR is always the base currency in the previous example when traded with the USD. For example, when you want to buy EUR and sell USD, you will buy the EUR/USD pair. Similarly, when you want to buy USD and sell EUR, you would sell the EUR/USD pair.

Commodities & Rare Metal Investing

Commodities are tangible assets and mostly natural resources, such as agricultural products, oil, natural gas, and precious metals. Commodities are considered a hedge against inflation, as they're not easily susceptible to public equity markets. The value of commodities rises and falls with supply and demand; higher demand for commodities results in higher prices, and therefore, investors make a profit. You have probably heard the mention of precious metals during economic uncertainty. Precious metals are stable during uncertainty because precious metals are considered a beneficial portfolio diversifier and hedge against inflation.

We are generally told to buy gold during these times. Although gold is the most well-known precious metal, it is not the only one out there for investors to add to their portfolios. If you desire to invest in precious metals, I recommend you learn about other options that may suit your portfolio beyond gold.

For instance, silver, platinum, and palladium are all commodities that can be added to your precious metals' portfolio, and each has its unique risks and opportunities. The CME Institute, an organization with the Chicago Mercantile Exchange, the world's largest and most diverse market for commodity trading and other derivatives, provides tons of webinars and videos you can leverage to learn more about commodities.

There are many ways to add this precious metal to your portfolio. I know many people who are very adamant about physically owning gold and silver plates. However, there are a plethora of approaches to investing in precious metals. Besides owning physical metal, investors can gain access through the derivatives market, metal ETFs, and mutual funds and invest in mining company stocks. While investing in rare-earth metals can be a great way to diversify your portfolio, investors should remember that these metals are still commodities, which means they're subject to fluctuations in global economic cycles. There are also global political and economic risks to consider. For example, China has now dominated the industry, creating risks around the pricing of the metals that impact the fortunes of global producers.

What's the difference between stocks and commodities? As we explained earlier, stocks are equities, meaning that the buyer of the stock owns a portion of the company represented by the stock, basically meaning you have ownership in future cash flows. Conversely, buying commodities allows the investor to own a tangible product.

Investors who buy stocks make money when the companies they invest in grow their business and increase profits, making stock in that company more desirable and increasing the stock price. Commodities rise in value simply when there is heightened demand for that particular commodity. Historically, stocks have outperformed precious metals in terms of investment—however, commodities such as precious metals provide stability, security, and protection against inflation.

Cryptocurrency Investing

Cryptocurrency is one of the most talked-about alternative investment vehicles. When he first began talking about it, my college buddies and I thought our friend Damu Winston was insane. However, we quickly realized that this required us to pay attention since ordinary people were becoming wealthy. In fact, Damu is the author of a book titled *I Don't Trust You: But Blockchain and Bitcoin Will Help.*

What is cryptocurrency? It is decentralized digital money based on blockchain technology—you may be familiar with the most popular versions, Bitcoin and Ethereum. A cryptocurrency allows you to perform certain functions, such as sending money to another person or using smart contracts that automatically execute after specific conditions are met.

You need a place to buy and store it; cryptocurrency exchanges are the most common places to purchase cryptocurrency, with several different exchanges to select from—the most popular being Coinbase, GDAx, and Bitfinex.

These exchanges let you purchase currencies like Bitcoin and Ethereum with your debit card. With most popular currencies, including Bitcoin, you can buy percentages of a coin, so you don't need to spend thousands of dollars to get in the game.

You also need a place to store your cryptocurrency. A cryptocurrency wallet is required to securely store the data in your cryptocurrency portfolio. You can have either a *software wallet* or a *hardware wallet.* Software wallets are necessary to enable active trading by making currency much more easily accessible. For example, when you sign up for a Coinbase account, you automatically receive a Coinbase software wallet. Hardware wallets are physical devices that look like USB drives and are considered more secure than software wallets. Therefore, you can use them for a currency you don't need to immediately or frequently access. For example, a software wallet is a checking account for cryptocurrency, whereas a hardware wallet is more like a safe.

How do cryptocurrencies differ from stocks? The most noticeable difference is that a stock is an ownership interest in a business backed by the company's assets and cash flow. In contrast, cryptocurrency, in most cases, is not supported by anything at all except for specialized stablecoins. The only thing moving crypto prices is speculation driven by human sentiment. As sentiment changes, prices shift, and in some cases, drastically.

With that being said, cryptocurrency is driven only by the belief that someone will buy it for more in the future, which is only partially true with stocks since they have underlying assets and cash flows to support the valuation. For example, if investors don't like a stock, they can sell it to cause the price to drop, but ultimately the company has to cease operating for the stock to lose value completely. Conversely, if crypto traders decide they don't want to own a cryptocurrency, it could plunge to zero due to not being backed by underlying assets or cash flow.

Another risk is political since countries could ban cryptocurrencies entirely, as China did in 2021. China announced new regulations prohibiting all cryptocurrency mining and transactions, condemning the technology as a threat to citizens' assets and a tool for facilitating criminal activities like money laundering. One of the reasons governments don't like it is because it presents an opportunity for individuals to avoid taxes. For example, individuals could potentially use a pseudonymous, decentralized platform to avoid generating records at traditional financial institutions to hide income from tax authorities.

Should you invest in cryptocurrency? It depends. I generally recommend that individuals not support anything they can't afford to lose. I don't recommend that anyone invest in cryptocurrency before meeting other financial goals such as unproductive consumer debt, investing employers' matched contributions to retirement accounts such as a 401(k), and having a portfolio allocation strategy.

Because cryptocurrency is relatively new, it is not yet firmly established as an asset class, and I think people should exercise caution. However, it could prove to be a substantial investment vehicle down the road, so it may be worth exploring.

With that being said, given its inherent risks, cryptocurrency might work better as a small allocation in your overall portfolio—no more than 10% but closer to five percent or less.

The exciting thing is that you don't have to invest directly in cryptocurrency to stake in the cryptocurrency market. Instead, many of the best index funds include publicly traded companies with some involvement with the industry by either mining crypto, being involved in the advancement of blockchain technology, or holding considerable amounts of crypto on their balance sheets—as Tesla does.

Chapter Nine
Taking Advantage of Cash Value Life Insurance

Life insurance is one of the most overlooked tools for wealth creation. Specifically, life insurance that has a cash value component. A cash value life insurance policy is a type of permanent life insurance policy with an investment feature that earns interest on the cash value portion of the policy. You can withdraw money from the cash value or take a loan using the cash value as collateral. Cash from the policy's cash value component is used to invest in other assets or cover certain expenses, including paying for emergencies, supplementing retirement income, and paying premiums should you become unable to do so. There's no limit to how you can use cash value. If you decide to end the policy, you can also take your cash value. If you terminate the policy with the insurer, you receive the cash value amount minus any surrender charge. This action ends the life insurance coverage. Surrender charges typically occur if you terminate the policy within the first several years of purchasing it. The surrender charge is a way for the insurer to cover the cost of issuing you the policy.

Like all insurance policies, there is a premium payment that policyholders are responsible for paying. However, only a portion of your insurance payment contributes to your cash value. Premium payments for cash value life insurance go three places:

- Into the policy's cash value
- To the cost of actually insuring you
- Toward policy fees and changes

The two main attributes of a cash value life insurance policy are the death benefit and cash value feature. In contrast, term life insurance only insures during a specified term and does not include a cash value feature. Another difference between the two is that term life is generally cheaper. Nevertheless, both have a death benefit. The death benefit is paid out to your beneficiaries when you pass away. The amount is called the "face value" of your policy or the amount of life insurance coverage. So, for example, a $250,000 whole life insurance policy would offer a death benefit protection that provides your family $250,000 of financial security if you were to pass away. Some advantages include replacing lost wages, benefits, Social Security, and any other compensation you would customarily expect to receive in the future.

Types of Permanent Life Insurance with a Cash Value Feature

There are two main types of permanent life insurance that include a cash value feature—whole life and universal life insurance policies. Whole life is an insurance policy guaranteed to remain in force for the insured's entire lifetime, provided required premiums are paid. Universal life insurance is permanent life insurance with an investment element and low premiums, which is similar to term life insurance. Most universal life insurance policies contain a flexible premium option. Both whole life and universal life have different variations that will be covered.

Whole Life Insurance

Whole life insurance is the most popular of the two. Whole life insurance is the simplest cash value policy type of permanent life insurance. Whole life insurance policyholders don't have to decide how the cash value is invested. Instead, the insurance company provides a fixed rate of return that determines how the cash value will grow.

Here's a summary of whole life insurance:

- Offers fixed monthly premiums, and premium payments don't change over time

- Provides a guaranteed death benefit
- Cash value accumulates at a minimum guaranteed rate
- Can receive company dividends that can be used to grow the cash value portion faster when placed in a cash value account
- Whole life insurance guarantees make it a pricier life insurance option than others

Another benefit of some whole life insurance coverage is the eligibility to receive dividends from the policy. You can use the dividends to pay up premiums or reinvest the dividends. The dividends are then used to purchase additional coverage, which enhances death benefit protection, increases cash value, and potentially leads to more dividends in the future. The amount of the dividend payout is correlated to the premiums, meaning the higher the dividend, the higher the premiums.

Guaranteed Whole Life Insurance

When Anthony "AJ" Johnson, a comedian and actor best known for his parts in "Friday" and "House Party," died, he didn't have life insurance. Fans were shocked to learn on social media that a GoFundMe account was created to cover his funeral expenses. One type of whole life insurance that would have prevented the stress of scrambling for funeral donations is guaranteed issue life insurance. These whole life policies are often called burial insurance. We too often receive a request to donate to a GoFundMe account because no one thought to have insurance to cover this expense. It is advisable to at least have this policy to ensure your family can cover your burial expenses during an already difficult and financially impactful time. With guaranteed issue life insurance, you can't be turned down, and the application process does not require a medical exam like many other policies. Often, they are available only in small coverage amounts, such as $10,000. Guaranteed issue life insurance can have a cash value benefit but is generally minimum due to the small size of the policy. One thing to keep in mind is that a guaranteed issue life insurance has a graded death benefit. This means your beneficiaries won't get the full payout if you pass away within a few years of buying the policy unless the death was due to an accident. Therefore, please make sure you understand all rules and stipulations before buying guaranteed issue life insurance.

Universal Life Insurance

Universal life insurance (ULI) policies are the most common cash-value life insurance policies available. However, not all universal life is the same, and some of them don't build cash value well, so make sure you understand what you're buying if cash value growth is your goal. Some types of universal life insurance policies offer the ability to accumulate greater cash value but also with some risk of loss. Other types of universal life policies give policyholders the option to adjust death benefits and premiums within certain parameters. Let's explore some of the policies out there to show the difference among universal life insurance types.

Guaranteed universal life insurance is a type of universal life insurance meant to last your entire life and to offer your beneficiaries a significant payout once you are "gone on to glory," as my aunt would say. You can select an age guarantee from 70 to 120. It is similar to whole life insurance because premiums are steady and will not increase at any given point, and the death benefit will not decrease. However, this means you must continue paying premiums or lose the policy. There is no market risk, and the policy will perform as usual, even if market interest rates are affected. The cash value accumulation may be minimal. Unlike many policies with significant cash value, there is no cash to cover premiums should you lapse in your ability to pay. Generally, it is the least expensive universal life insurance option. Guaranteed universal life insurance is purchased to cover your final expenses and estate taxes. Some policies allow you to add a living benefits rider to provide compensation while alive should you develop a critical illness. The downside is that the guaranteed life insurance policy is inflexible compared to certain life insurance policies that allow you to adjust your premium and death benefit. The guaranteed universal does not allow for such changes.

Another variation of universal life is **indexed universal life insurance**. Indexed ULI can be a great flexible mechanism for wealth building with the benefit of tax-free gains. Generally, this type of policy is great for someone with a large upfront investment that can be maximized over a longer term. With an indexed ULI, the growth of your cash value is connected to gains and losses in an index, such as the S&P 500. Unlike guaranteed ULI, you can adjust premiums and death benefits within certain parameters. Some downsides include caps on returns and no guarantees regarding premium amounts or market returns.

The last ULI policy type we will cover is **variable universal life insurance**. The variable ULI combines a savings component with a separate death benefit. Each year, the life insurer deducts what it needs to cover mortality and administrative costs, usually ranging from 0.05% to 2%. The rest remains in separate accounts to earn further interest. The cash value growth is tied to subaccounts similar to mutual funds, including stocks and bonds, that contain investments you choose. These investments can lead to significant increases based on the market's volatility. Similar to indexed ULI, you can generally change your premium and death benefits within set limits. Policyholders can withdraw from the cash value or borrow funds. Still, the policy does require a minimum cash level that will require additional premiums if the account drops below that amount. The downside is that your investment decisions could result in losing money in your cash value should the market not perform and can have a higher administrative cost.

How do whole life and universal life insurance differ?

The biggest difference for policyholders between whole and universal life is the guarantees. For instance, whole life has a guaranteed death benefit, stable premiums, and consistent cash value. This growth in cash value comes from annual dividends credited to policies. Universal life provides flexibility instead of guarantees. The policy's flexibility allows you to pay more or less each year for the policy, which causes both death benefit and cash value to fluctuate. In addition, universal life policies are credited based on market performance and interest rates rather than dividend payments. This can lead to an underfunded universal life policy, causing premiums to increase proportionately. If premiums cannot be met, the policy can terminate.

However, with whole life insurance, you pay higher premiums for the guarantees you are given. Therefore, an equivalent universal life policy will cost less but also comes with the risk previously outlined.

Ways to withdraw cash from a life insurance policy

There are four main ways to access the money in your cash value policy. The first is to take a tax-free withdrawal for the money you have paid into the policy. Any amount beyond what you have paid into the policy is subject to being taxed as income. Withdrawals also reduce the death benefit of the policy.

The second way to withdraw from your policy is to take a loan. A loan from your policy is essentially like borrowing from yourself—you can generally borrow up to the cash value built up on your policy, including premiums and accrued interest. The borrowed amount is not considered taxable income. The outstanding loan is deducted from the death benefit if you die before the loan is paid back. Your loan amount accrues interest until it's paid back in full. The interest on a policy loan may be fixed or a variable rate calculated by the insurer based on current market rates. State law often dictates the maximum policy loan interest rate. For example, California and Texas let insurance companies charge a maximum fixed rate of up to 8% yearly. If you don't repay the loan amount and you pass away, the insurance company subtracts the outstanding loan balance (including interest) from the life insurance payout to your beneficiaries. Some policyholders use their cash value this way and intend for their beneficiaries to get a reduced payout.

The policyholder uses the cash value as collateral versus physically withdrawing cash from their account. This means the cash value is still growing and acquiring equity even while borrowing against it to invest in assets like real estate. Essentially, your dollar is working double because you have two assets simultaneously working for you. The insurance company gives you a loan up to some function of your cash value, between 70–90%. The insurance company holds the policy as collateral; you lose the cash value associated with what you have borrowed if you default. The remaining 10–30% would be reflected on your account as a lower net surrender value, or NSV. The NSV is the specific sum of money a life insurance company will award to a policyholder during a voluntary termination of a life insurance policy before it reaches maturity. For example, if you had a cash value of $100,000 and borrowed $80,0000, your NSV would be $20,000. However, the full $100,000 is still accruing and compounding interest.

Once you have borrowed from your policy, the liquidity will come in the form of a check you will take to the bank to use for your investment. You would be subject to interest, but this is often lower than the interest your money makes in the cash value.

Let's now compare this to borrowing against a 401(k). With a 401(k), you are borrowing your actual money. Therefore, the institution deducts the money from your account and sends you a check that you must pay back relatively quickly. In contrast, with a cash value policy, your cash serves as collateral for the loan, and you continue to accumulate interest growing your full cash value.

The death benefit comes with a cash value policy, like whole life insurance. Plus, the loan-to-value amount is much less for your 401(k)—usually no more than 50% loan-to-value and no more than $50,000. Also, you will owe tax on the balance for the early withdrawal penalty if you leave your company early and don't pay it back. And you have five years to pay it back, compared with a life insurance loan that can be paid back over the policyholder's life. The loan should be paid before then—if it isn't, the amount will be deducted from the death benefit. Please remember that a cash value life insurance policy loan still requires you to pay interest just like you would to any other financial institution. The good news is that the rates are usually fixed, and there are typically no penalties for early withdrawal. Also, when purchasing a cash value life insurance policy, you'll need to pay your premium every month or year. If you don't have the funds available, you can lose your policy.

The third way to withdraw funds is to surrender your life insurance policy or cancel it. The policy would no longer insure you, but any equity built up from the policy's cash value portion and any accumulated interest will be paid to you. Keep in mind that any outstanding loans or unpaid premiums will be deducted beforehand. You may also be subject to any fees from early termination and taxes.

How do you use your cash value policy to buy real estate?

If you're looking to finance a real estate investment, a lesser-known option allows you to borrow from your life insurance policy. This concept, called infinite banking, was popularized in the book *Becoming Your Own Banker* by Nelson Nash. Infinite banking means borrowing from a cash value insurance policy instead of depending on banks or loans. While there are things to consider, it can be a viable way to grow your wealth through real estate, tax-deferred.

There are two ways you can invest in several states using cash value life insurance. The first way is to buy relief from the policy and finance cash-flowing real estate assets. The second way is to qualify with a lender by using cash value and the policy as collateral. I like to call this the double play strategy because the cash value is working in two places. The cash is still in your insurance account working for you, while the money you borrowed generates income for you with real estate. Since real estate has created more millionaires than any asset class, this could be an effective strategy. Real estate also allows you to take advantage of specific tax write-offs that come with owning real estate. The disadvantages are that this increases your debt load, and should you not be able to pay, creditors may come after the cash value. Finally, this type of funding can be difficult to qualify for.

How to build an effective cash value policy?

Let's be clear: no life insurance policy generates immediate cash value unless you add a rider, such as a paid-up addition or an enhanced liquidity rider. Cash value life insurance grows over time and at a steady pace. First, let's discuss how you might build an effective cash value policy. An index universal life insurance policy is the best policy to maximize cash accumulation. Whole life is better if you need to access the cash immediately.

Leverage Paid-Up Additions

If your goal is to build high early cash value, you'll want to find permanent insurance providers that allow you to leverage a paid-up additions rider (PUA or PUAR). A rider allows the owner of the life insurance contract to make additional contributions to the policy, resulting in the addition of paid-up life insurance, which increases the death benefit and cash value. This rider, also known as an *enricher rider*, or *additional life insurance rider*, is an essential component of a properly designed dividend-paying whole life insurance policy focused on cash value accumulation. Paid-up additions are exclusive to a specific type of whole life insurance policies. Including a paid-up additions rider in your policy allows you to make purchases of paid-up additional insurance with no proof of insurability, increasing the cash value and death benefit proportionately. Moreover, the additional paid-up life insurance can earn life insurance dividends, which compounds the cash value growth inside the policy.

Avoid the MEC

However, it should be noted that you can only put so much money into your policy. An overfunded policy transforms the policy into a modified endowment contract (MEC). If your policy reaches these limits, you will lose some of the tax advantages of permanent life insurance. However, most insurance providers will communicate when you reach these limits and give you time to remedy the situation.

Paid-Up Additions Dividend Option

The paid-up additions dividend option is not to be confused with paid-up additions. Whereas the rider to the whole life policy must be added, the dividend option to purchase paid-up additions is a distinct feature of the policy.

Life insurance dividends allow you to choose different options, such as taking the cash out or buying additional paid-up life insurance. It is important to reiterate that additional paid-in-full whole life insurance using policy dividends is separate from the paid-up additions rider. Therefore, the dividend option could be a great path to maximizing cash value growth in your policy.

When the two paid-up additions options—the dividend paid-up additions option and the particular paid-up additions feature—are used together, the combination can supercharge cash value investment over the long term. The following life insurance companies offer paid-up additions:

- American United Life
- Guardian Life
- Lafayette Life
- MassMutual
- Mutual Trust Life
- New York Life
- Northwestern Mutual
- Ohio National
- Penn Mutual

Potential Drawback to PUAs

One of the main drawbacks of using a PUA rider is the fees. As we previously outlined, paid-up additions can be defined as additional insurance that is paid in full at the time of purchase, minus a deducted amount the insurance company charges as a load fee against paid-up additions. The typical load fee varies by the insurance company and can range from 4% to 9%, with certain questionable insurers reserving the right to raise fees to 20%.

Enhanced Liquidity Rider

The enhanced liquidity rider gives you increased access to the cash value portion of your universal life insurance policy. It does this by waiving a specified percentage of your surrender charges, which are the fees you pay to access your cash value before the specified time. Increased access to your cash benefit can be very helpful in an emergency.

Understand how long it takes for your policy to generate cash

As I said earlier, no policy generates cash value immediately. However, if the cash value is your goal, it is important to understand how it accumulates and when you will start seeing some future ROI. During your insurance policy's early years, a larger percentage of your premium is invested and allocated to the cash value account. This cash value can grow quickly in the early years. However, in the later years, the cash value accumulation begins to slow as you grow older, and more of the premium is applied to the insurance cost. As you get older, the risks and cost of insuring your life increase for the life insurance company. This also means that the older you are, the more it costs to purchase a term life policy. That's why it is best to get it early.

Cash value growth also depends on the type of insurance you select. For example, whole life insurance provides guaranteed fixed cash value account growth according to a formula determined by the insurance companies. On the other hand, universal life policies accumulate cash value based on current interest rates in investments. Finally, variable life insurance policies invest funds in subaccounts that function like mutual funds. As a result, the cash value in these accounts may fluctuate, rise or fall according to the performance of the attached subaccounts.

The break-even period generally ranges from 6–12 years. The break-even period is when your total cash value has caught up to your cumulative premium. Historically, this break-even period has been closer to five to eight years. Please keep in mind that fees are industry averages. For example, I have a business partner who was able to structure a cash value insurance policy that allowed him to accelerate cash growth and earn money within the first three years. Of course, this all depends on how your policy is structured. Be sure to speak to multiple agents to evaluate what best works for you.

What happens to the cash value when you die?

The bottom line is that the cash value in your policy goes back to the insurance company when you die. Policyholders can only use the cash value while alive, which means your beneficiaries will not receive any of the cash portion of the policy. They're only entitled to the death benefit. For example, Mary has a whole life insurance policy with a $500,000 death benefit. However, she aggressively built cash value into her insurance policy over 30 years. When Mary died, she had $600,000 of cash value built up. The insurance company will absorb the $600,000 cash value, and Mary's beneficiaries will receive the $500,000 death benefit. In this scenario, it may have been best for Mary to use some of the cash value in the policy before her death.

On the other hand, if Mary had taken a loan from the policy and not paid the loan back, that amount plus interest would have been deducted from the death benefit. The bottom line is that you should work with your financial advisers to understand the implications of having cash value with your insurance policy. You must begin with the end in mind, meaning you must decide whether leveraging cash value during your life or the death benefit is more important and downspout the pros and cons with a long-term strategy.

Another option would have been for Mary to have structured the policy differently. For example, some insurance policies allow you to increase your death benefit as you build cash value, requiring you to have a paid insurance rider attached to your policy. For example, suppose you have accumulated sizable cash value over the life of your cash value life insurance policy and don't believe you will use the funds yourself. In that case, you may leave your beneficiaries a more considerable death benefit. Essentially, you would tell your insurance broker that you would like to increase the death benefit in exchange for your policy's cash value. The objective of this strategy would be to completely drain the cash value and transfer the full amount over to the death benefit portion of the insurance policy. So, for example, if you had a $250,000 policy with $100,000 of cash value accumulated, you would now have a $350,000 policy with the corresponding death benefit.

Chapter Summary/Key Takeaways

This chapter focused on the importance of life insurance policies and the role they play in wealth creation. These policies are an untapped resource when you need money for real estate purchases and other acquisitions you desire to make. There are several different types of life insurance policies, and in this chapter, the focus is on cash value, whole life, and universal life insurance.

Cash value insurance is a type of permanent life insurance that allows you to use its cash value or to take a loan from the cash value to finance things such as premiums or emergencies. On the other hand, whole life insurance is one of the most popular policies because it has a lot of value and features, such as a guaranteed death benefit. Under the umbrella of whole life insurance are other insurance policies, such as burial and guaranteed issue life insurance. Lastly, there is universal life insurance, which allows for greater cash value along with some risk of loss. Under universal life insurance, there is a variable, index, and guaranteed universal life insurance. Each of these policies has its benefits as well as some downsides. Which type of policy will work for your financial goals all depends on your needs and your risk tolerance.

In addition, the cash value from these policies can help you with investment opportunities such as real estate purchases. Knowing how to withdraw your insurance policy's cash value and use it will help you achieve your investment goals. Also, understanding how to build up your cash value, knowing how long it takes to build cash value, leveraging paid-up additions, and avoiding the MEC will assist you in making sure you achieve your financial goals. Knowing how to maximize your cash value in life insurance policies will get you on the path toward financial freedom and stability.

Chapter Ten
Preserving Wealth Across Generations

So, you've worked hard to make the right investment decisions, secure assets, and create a comfortable life. You have also decided that you want to share the wealth with your spouse, children, grandchildren, and beyond when you pass away. Therefore, you decide that you want to create "generational wealth." You may even believe that simply creating the assets or maybe going the extra step to add your loved ones as beneficiaries on your insurance policy is sufficient. Sadly, these actions alone will not create generational wealth. The best mechanism to create generational wealth is by creating a family trust. You have probably read articles about acclaimed artist Pablo Picasso or viewed his artwork in a museum, but you may not have heard he died without an estate plan.

Estate planning is the preparation of tasks that manage an individual's assets in the event of death or incapacitation. When Picasso died in 1973 at 91, he had amassed a fortune in homes, cash, artwork, and government bonds. Sadly, he had not done any estate planning. It took six years and $30 million in legal fees to finally settle his estate. The costly and lengthy process of settling his estate could have all been avoided with a family trust.

A family trust is a great tool for managing your wealth over multiple generations and passing that wealth to beneficiaries according to your specifications. In addition, the trust allows you to instruct how your assets will be managed, who has access to them, when distributions are made, and under what conditions and timelines.

So, what is a trust? In general, a trust is a legal vehicle that holds assets on behalf of a beneficiary. The trust outlines when those assets are distributed based on specific conditions outlined in the trust documents.

If the ultimate beneficiaries of the living trust are the family members of the person who created the trust, it will often be referred to as a family trust. On the other hand, if those beneficiaries include friends, charities, or other nonfamily members, the trust is typically referred to as just a living trust. This chapter will focus on family trust.

A trust has three key parts: the grantor, the trustee, and the beneficiaries. A grantor establishes the trust and funds it by transferring assets into it. These assets include bank accounts, stocks, bonds, real estate, business entities, intellectual property, and other valuables. The trustee or trustees will administer the trust on behalf of the beneficiaries, who receive financial benefits from the trust according to the rules outlined in the trust documents. As previously mentioned, typically, in a family trust, the grantor and beneficiaries are related, such as parents or grandparents, who might name children, grandchildren, and other family members as beneficiaries.

Basic Trust Structure

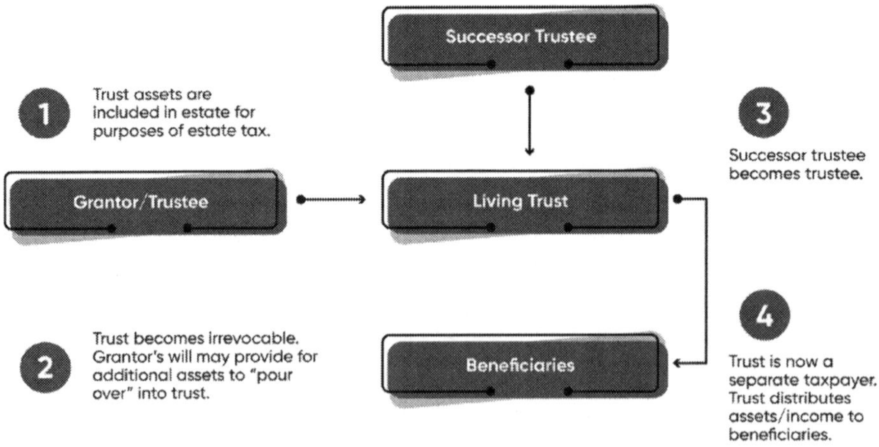

Why have a trust? Having a trust in place can offer peace of mind that your assets will be managed according to your wishes, both during your life and after you die. You might ask, is having a will and testament or letters outlining my wishes enough? Unfortunately, wills can be contested and go through a lengthy probate process. And letters are not sufficient legal documentation since they have not been certified, and legitimacy is often questioned. Remember the famous actor Chadwick Boseman from the movie Black Panther? After his untimely death, his estate worth more than three million dollars went through a lengthy probate process. This meant that his wife and family could not receive money from his estate until this process was concluded. The results were that his wife received $1.15 million, his family received $1.15 million, and the government, through the probate process, took the remaining $1.15 million. This could have been prevented had Chadwick had a solid trust in place.

The trust has benefits for both creators and beneficiaries. Some of the benefits of interest include:

- Passing assets to beneficiaries without going through probate courts, as we mentioned earlier with the Chadwick Boseman estate.
- Setting aside assets for the care of your minor children should you pass away, which can include children with special needs.
- Creating a plan to manage assets should you become incapacitated in any way.
- Establishing requirements to ensure beneficiaries manage inheritance responsibly, along with mechanisms to prevent them from squandering their hard-earned assets.
- Potentially reducing estate and gift taxes during your life and beyond.
- Creating peace of mind that your loved ones will be taking care of you when you can no longer do it yourself.

The types of assets you may transfer to a trust include:

- Real property, including personal property, land, and rental property
- Deposit accounts held by banks and other financial institutions
- Investments, including stocks, bonds, treasury accounts, cryptocurrency, etc.
- Business entities and other business assets
- Intellectual property, such as music royalties, inventions, published books, art, and other creative royalties
- Collectibles and valuables

Although creating trust documents with a lawyer is a great first step, a trust isn't meaningful until it has been funded. Funding a trust occurs when you transfer assets into the trust and are under the trustee's control.

There are several types of trusts, but trusts typically fall into two broad categories: revocable and irrevocable.

Revocable trusts, also called living trusts, allow you to maintain control of your assets during your lifetime. For example, if you go through a divorce, acquire new wealth, or need to liquidate assets, you may need to adjust the terms of your trust. On the other hand, once an irrevocable trust is created, you cannot change them in any way. For example, if you transfer real estate or business assets that you own to the trust, you cannot modify this in any way. So why would you want to create an irrevocable trust? Individuals and families create an irrevocable trust to safeguard assets from creditors, beneficiaries, or even their governments. An irrevocable trust protects your assets from estate and gift taxes, which can appeal to large estates with millions to hundreds of millions of dollars in assets.

In addition to the two broad categories of trusts previously mentioned, a variety of specialty family trusts and structures can be created in your estate plan to meet your needs.

Some of these specialty trusts include:

- Testamentary trust
- Marital trust
- Spouse limited access trust
- Bypass trust
- Special needs trust
- Life insurance trust
- Dynasty trust/legacy trust

Testamentary trust

Barry, a wealthy physician with lots of assets, dies suddenly in an accident. He had three kids from a previous marriage. He recently married a woman with two children of her own. Barry doesn't have a will or any estate planning whatsoever. The fight over his assets consumes much of the fortune Barry created with legal fees and taxes. Barry would have benefited from having created a testamentary trust, better known as a last will and testament.

A testamentary trust provides for the distribution of all or part of an estate and often precedes from a life insurance policy held on the person establishing the trust. A testamentary trust is created for young children, beneficiaries with disabilities, or others who may inherit large sums of money. A trustee will manage assets on behalf of the trust's beneficiaries until a specific time period or event, such as graduating from college. The testamentary trust differs from other trusts created during your lifetime, as the trust is not completed until after you have passed away. With this type of trust, the probate courts play a role. From the moment you die until the expiration of the testamentary trust, the probate court ensures the trust is being handled properly, which can add legal fees. Once again, compared to a living trust, the disadvantage of the testamentary trust is that it does not avoid probate. Probate is the court-supervised legal process that verifies that a will is legitimate and appoints an executor who will administer the estate and distribute assets to the beneficiaries.

The probate process can be time-consuming and costly depending on the assets that need to be distributed. Also, going through probate will make the trust a public record. This can draw unwanted attention from creditors or other interested parties.

Creating a testamentary trust can range from simple to complex. There are many resources to create this type of trust online; however, it is advisable to consult an attorney to ensure the document is prepared correctly and assets are distributed properly. Depending on your situation, a testamentary trust may be sufficient. Still, most estate planners would recommend anyone with assets and a positive net worth to consider some form of a living trust.

Testamentary Trust Formation & Probate Process

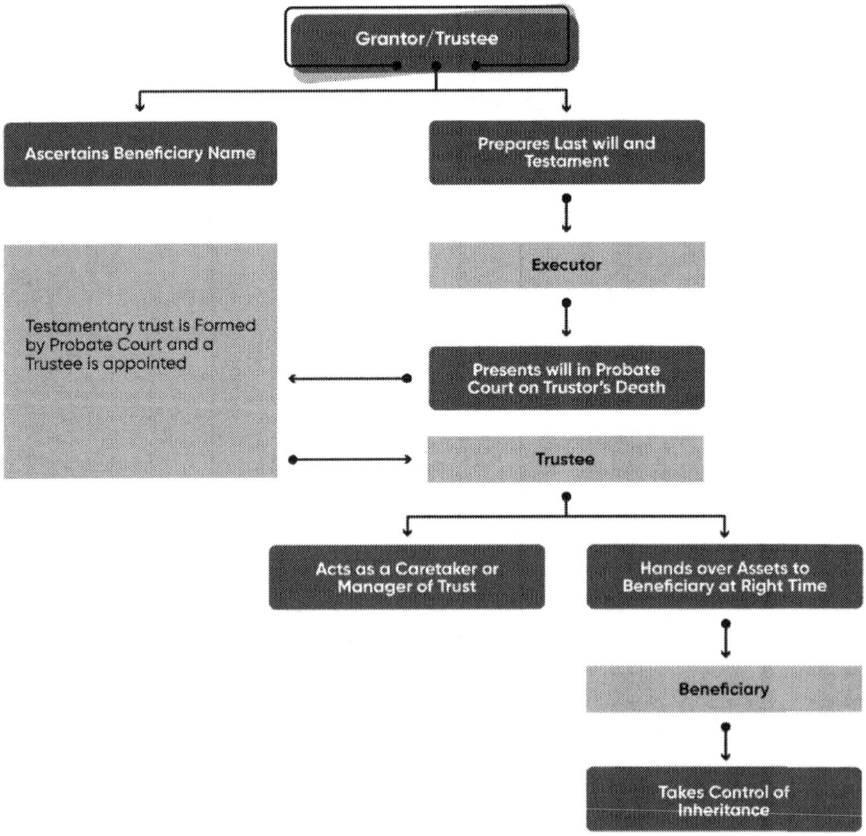

Marital trust

Although it's not a desirable topic for married couples, you or your spouse will inevitably pass away. What can you do to ensure your spouse is cared for when you pass away, and inherited assets are properly managed?

The answer could take the form of a marital trust. A marital trust is a revocable trust that belongs to the surviving spouse. This trust has terms that can be changed by the person who established the trust. A marital trust has an assortment of benefits for the trust's grantor and beneficiary, including asset allocation, asset protection from creditors or spouse(s) of the surviving spouse, tax benefits, and peace of mind. In addition, when the surviving spouse dies, the assets in the trust are not included as part of their estate, which would reduce taxes. Although marital trusts have many advantages, a key benefit is that it doubles the couple's estate tax exemption limits. In 2022, the estate tax limit was $12 million, so the marital trust essentially doubled that amount to $24 million. For example, suppose the grantor passes $10 million to a surviving spouse through a marital trust. In that case, the surviving spouse still has a remaining $14 million to transfer to the couple's children and grandchildren because of the doubling of tax limits from using the marital trust. A marital trust is also beneficial because it can provide tax-free income to the surviving spouse.

It is also important to note that only a surviving spouse can be a beneficiary of a marital trust; once the surviving spouse passes, the remaining assets are to pass along to whoever the grantor specified. The downsides of a marital trust are that they are irrevocable, and it is extremely difficult to change or dissolve the terms. Also, they must be set up and funded properly, which could be a lengthy process. You should work with an experienced attorney specializing in this type of trust.

Spouse limited access trust (SLAT)

A SLAT is an irrevocable trust created by one spouse for the benefit of the other spouse during their lifetime. The grantor of the trust makes an irrevocable gift of assets to the SLAT, with their spouse and descendants being the beneficiaries. This allows the couple to take advantage of the current lifetime gift tax exemption amounts (~$12M per individual) by transferring assets out of both spouses' taxable estate while still having direct access to those assets through your spouse.

Though, keep in mind that the current large gift and estate tax exemptions are due to change on January 1, 2026. This type of trust also provides asset protection for your spouse and beneficiaries through creditor protection while simultaneously allowing your spouse to benefit from the assets in the trust. SLATs are considered a grantor trust, which means the grantor is responsible for paying federal income taxes. When the grantor does not pay the taxes, this is called a SLANT—spousal lifetime access non-grantor trust.

There are some disadvantages and risks associated, so be sure to have a good attorney drafting this type of trust. The IRS may view it as spouses gifting to themselves if you don't create the legal documents in different jurisdictions and name different trustees. In the case of divorce, the ex-spouse can still benefit from the trust assets, while the creating spouse could lose access.

SLAT Trust Formation

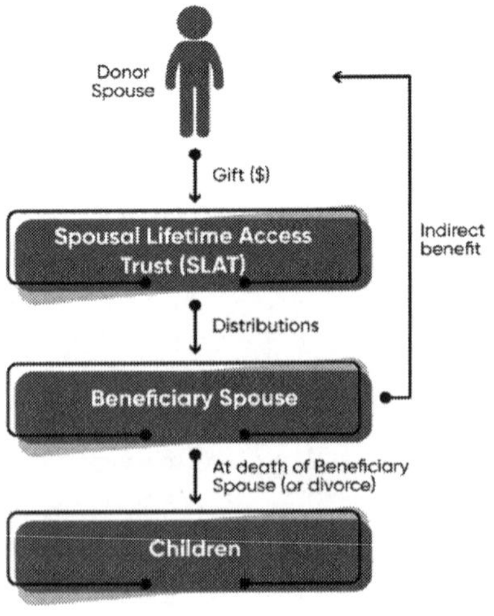

Bypass trust

A bypass or "AB" trust allows married couples to avoid estate tax on assets when one spouse passes away.

When one spouse dies, the trust is split into two separate trusts. The first part is a marital trust or "A" trust; the second is a bypass, family, or "B" trust. In this way, the marital trust belongs to the surviving spouse and is revocable. Meanwhile, the family trust or "B" trust is irrevocable. When the first spouse passes away, their share of the estate goes into the family or "B" trust. This way, the surviving spouse doesn't own those assets but can access the trust during their lifetime to receive income from it. At the same time, the surviving spouse has complete control over part A or the marital trust, which allows them to spend, sell, or transfer assets at their discretion. In this type of trust, the surviving spouse may be the trustee or appoint someone else as trustee of the bypass trust.

Bypass Trust Formation

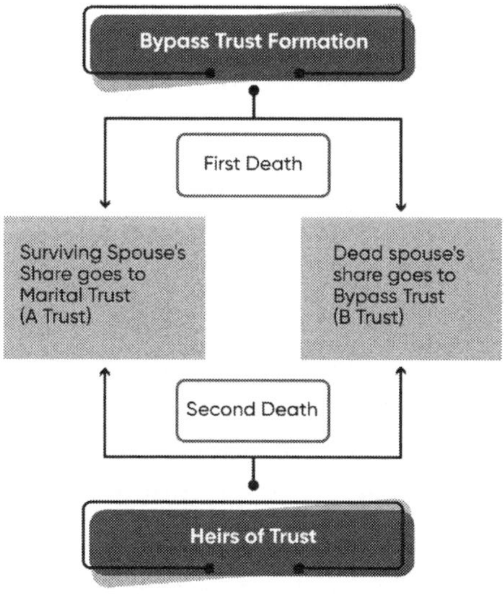

When speaking with an estate planner or attorney, you might also hear bypass trust used interchangeably with spousal limited access trust. The difference between a SLAT and a bypass trust is that a SLAT is funded while both spouses are alive, while a bypass trust is funded at the death of either spouse.

The appeal of the SLAT is that it can be a more flexible option that can be done while you are still living since tax laws and exemptions could change when you die. The benefits of a bypass trust are that it can minimize federal, state, and estate taxes for married couples with substantial assets. While assets in the marital trust that the surviving spouse holds are subject to federal or state estate tax, the family trust or portion of that trust's assets up to an annual exemption limit is not subject to federal estate taxes.

Additionally, holding assets in a bypass trust allows the surviving spouse to avoid probate. The disadvantages of the bypass trust are that they can be very costly and time-consuming. It requires a special eyes estate planning attorney specializing in this type of trust to manage the process. Also, such a trust requires ongoing maintenance, in which the surviving spouse needs to keep records of how the trust uses assets. However, a trustee can be named to manage these duties for a fee. There may be other limitations for the surviving spouse depending on how the trust is setup.

Special needs trust

If you have a child or loved one with special needs, you're probably wondering how to ensure their financial needs are being taken care of. One strategy is to set up a special needs trust. The special needs trust is created to provide for disabled or critically ill beneficiaries. These beneficiaries may or may not rely on government assistance. However, this type of trust is generally set up to preserve eligibility for Medicaid and supplemental Social Security benefits. Essentially, the trust will supplement government benefits for the beneficiary without replacing them. The trust is necessary because certain assets could disqualify your beneficiary from receiving government benefits.

For example, while owning a home and a car does not affect eligibility for Medicare or SSI, monetary gifts you may leave to your beneficiary would disqualify them. You can avoid this problem by placing financial assets and property into a special needs trust.

Similarly to other types of trusts, assets in the trust are managed by a trustee and not considered part of your loved one's assets.

These assets in the trust are used to pay for physical rehabilitation, caregivers, medical expenses, transportation, education, and other qualified needs. Specialty trusts are created just like any other trust, with the grantor funding the trust and selecting trustees to manage and oversee the distribution of assets according to the beneficiary's best interest. There are two main types of special needs trusts: an individual trust and a pooled special needs trust. Pooled trusts differ from individual special needs trusts because they are typically run by a nonprofit organization that pulls the resources from a group of families to invest the funds. The nonprofit then spends the money on behalf of each beneficiary. A special needs trust has specific qualifications that must be met or risk preventing the beneficiary from receiving public benefits. Generally, you can create a special needs trust to help your loved one with mental illness or addiction problems.

Additionally, here are some other regulations that apply to a specialties trust:

- The trust has to be created before the beneficiary turns 65.
- The funds in the trust cannot be used for food or housing expenses.
- The special needs trust is irrevocable, so creditors cannot access funds.
- Upon the death of the beneficiary, the trustee must transfer the remaining assets to other beneficiaries or the beneficiary's estate.

While the special needs trust has several rules, it does have a couple of advantages. As mentioned earlier, the special needs trust can help pay for expenses while keeping the beneficiary eligible for government assistance. Additionally, the special needs trust funds are tax deductible and protected from creditors and legal judgment.

On the other hand, some disadvantage to the special needs trust is as follows:

- The beneficiary lacks control of the funds since the trustee controls how their money is spent. The beneficiary must request funds from the trustee, and the trustee has full discretion on whether or not to honor the request.
- The trust must pay back Medicaid upon the beneficiary's death, often wiping out the remaining funds.

Special Needs Trust Formation

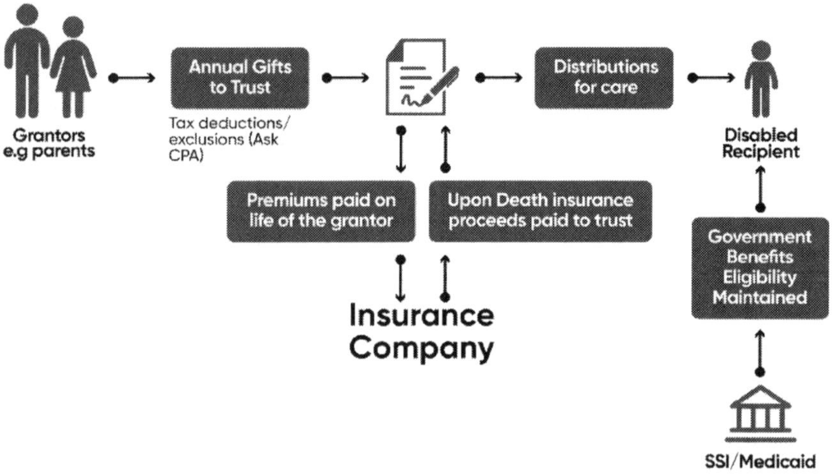

Life insurance trust

One concern you might have if you have a large life insurance policy is that the payout may cause estate taxes for your loved ones. Therefore, you may want to ensure that the policy's benefits do not pay out to your taxable estate. You can avoid this by creating a life insurance trust.

A life insurance trust is a trust that owns the eventual proceeds of any life insurance policies you own. By creating a life insurance trust, you no longer own the policy; the trust is not the owner.

Individuals who secure a life insurance trust are worried about the insurance policy payout increasing the size of their assets and consequently owing taxes. However, this is only a concern if your estate is worth more than the $12,000,000 federal exemption that exists today. These exemptions could be lower on the state inheritance tax. While these thresholds could change, you don't need to worry about making a life insurance trust unless you think the payout will bring your estate beyond the tax exemption range. This type of trust may also be a good strategy for special needs children who may require long-term care after you pass away. This becomes a way to fund a revocable special needs trust. Life insurance proceeds are not taxed as they go into the trust, and because the trust owns those assets, it may preserve eligibility for government benefits. While a life insurance trust can be created with a term life insurance policy or a permanent life insurance policy, they are typically designed with a permanent whole life policy with a guaranteed death benefit.

This is because trusts with a term insurance policy become problematic if the term ends before the insured person dies. This means the trust is left unfunded with nothing to distribute to beneficiaries. Also, permanent universal life insurance policies can be problematic because a death benefit amount isn't guaranteed, which means the trust could be left underfunded.

To establish a life insurance trust, you must first create an irrevocable trust, naming a trustee. Then it would be best if you transferred the policy into the trust, and the trust becomes the policy owner. This means that you no longer have any control over the policy, except according to the terms of the trust, which will determine who has control, who will benefit from the trust, and how funds will be distributed to beneficiaries in the event of your death. The trust must follow three basic rules:

- It is irrevocable.
- It must have a trustee that is not you.
- The trust must exist for three years before your death.

These rules are how the IRS ensures that you have no control over the policy after transfer to the trust and prohibits last-minute transfers to avoid estate taxes. The IRS will include the policy in your taxable estate if you do not follow these basic rules. However, you can still pay the premium on the policy or give money to someone else to pay it, but be careful to avoid gift taxes! If you think this is a viable option for you, contact a credible estate lawyer. The disadvantage to this type of trust is that you may need access to the cash value of your life insurance policy at some point. You would not have this option by putting it into an irrevocable life insurance trust. A revocable trust can be changed, but there may be significant legal fees.

Life Insurance Trust Formation

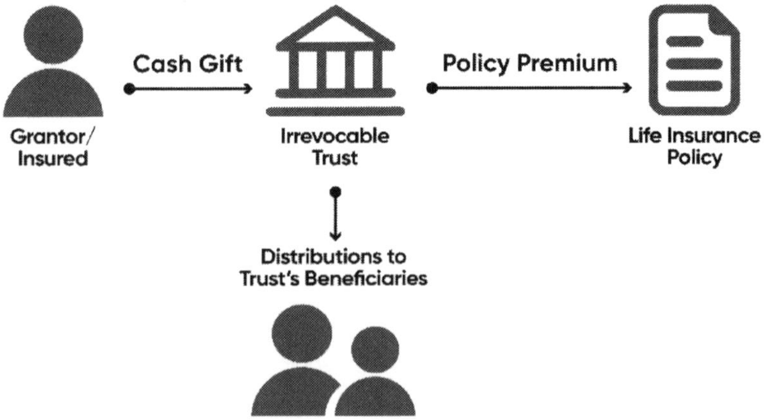

Dynasty trust/legacy trust

The term generational wealth has become a social media buzzword. However, unless you have created a structure and mechanisms with rules governing how your wealth will be distributed over time, you are not creating generational wealth.

To establish wealth for several generations, you may consider creating what is known as a dynasty trust. A dynasty trust is a long-term trust created to pass wealth from generation to generation without incurring transfer taxes, such as estate gift taxes. This type of trust allows wealthy families to take advantage of what is known as generation-skipping tax exemptions. As of 2023, the exemption threshold is about $12.9 million. For the trust to be considered a dynasty trust, it must be kept alive, meaning beneficiaries cannot deplete the accounts. In addition, dynasty trusts are irrevocable, and the terms cannot be changed once funded. The key difference between a dynasty trust and a traditional trust is time. Another benefit to a dynasty trust is that it allows you to protect assets for a long duration of time because the assets are not included in the beneficiaries' taxable estates since the trust owns the assets. This also leads to asset protection since creditors in divorce courts cannot go after the assets held by the trust.

With the dynasty trust, you can appoint a beneficiary to serve as a trustee; however, many trusts typically appoint a bank or a financial institution as a trustee of the dynasty trust.

Like other trusts, the trustee is responsible for trust oversight and ensuring assets are distributed to beneficiaries per the terms of the trust. Unlike many other trusts, the next generation of children will assume a beneficiary role when the last named beneficiary passes away, which continues according to the state's rules. For example, in Nevada, a dynasty trust can last up to 365 years, but in California, 90 years is the duration. The duration of time varies by state.

Here, the below 21 states allow dynasty trusts:

- Alaska
- Delaware
- District of Columbia
- Hawaii
- Idaho
- Illinois
- Kentucky
- Maine
- Maryland
- Michigan
- Missouri
- Nebraska
- New Hampshire
- New Jersey
- North Carolina
- Ohio
- Pennsylvania
- Rhode Island
- South Dakota
- Virginia
- Wisconsin

The advantages of a dynasty trust are that it can be a great option for families seeking to transfer wealth from generation to generation.

In addition, it can help families with sizable estates transfer wealth while avoiding estate and inheritance taxes. The downside to a dynasty trust is that it is irrevocable. This means that once it is set up, the terms of the trust cannot be amended. This means that changing family dynamics and asset structures may cause a dynasty trust not to be a good fit. Finally, dynasty trusts can be expensive, ranging from $3,000 to more than $30,000, depending on complexity.

Dynasty Trust Formation & Benefits

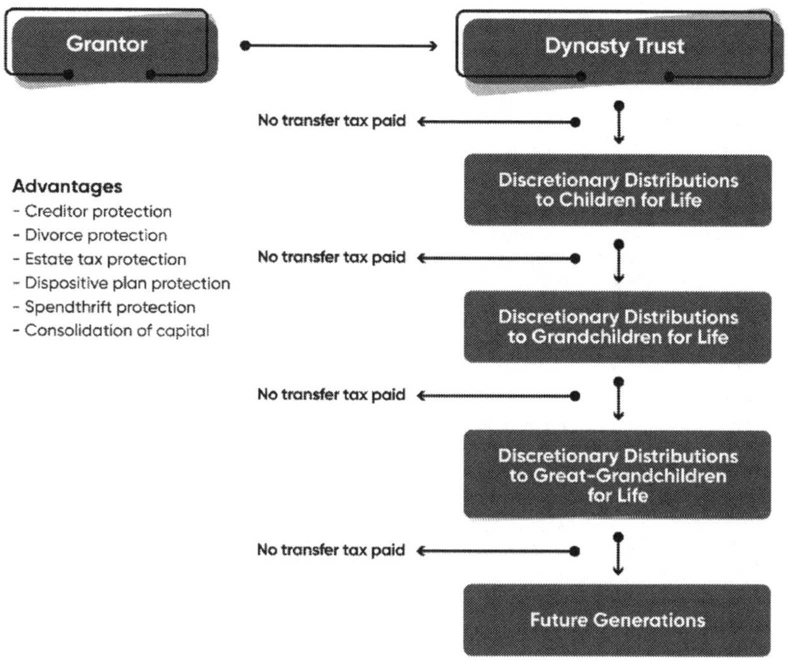

Chapter Summary/Key Takeaways

Establishing a trust for your family is a necessary step in estate planning and a crucial component of creating generational wealth. A living trust offers many benefits beyond a will since wills can be contested and go through a court process known as probate. Creating a trust allows you to dictate the wishes for your hard-earned assets and gives you peace of mind that your family is taken care of financially. Your financial situation, family dynamics, and goals will determine the kind of trust you will need.

The types of trusts discussed in this chapter are family, testamentary, marital, spouse limited access, bypass, special needs, life insurance, and dynasty/legacy. A family trust allows the beneficiaries to inherit funds after the person who established it dies. A testamentary trust is another name for a last will and testament and is enacted once the individual who establishes the trust passes away. Marital trusts are created for the surviving spouse so that they can use the trust as tax-free income once one spouse passes away. A spouse limited access trust is ideal for asset protection from creditors, and the spouses can transfer taxable assets into this trust. A bypass trust allows a surviving spouse to avoid estate taxes when the other spouse passes away and is funded when one individual dies, compared to while they are alive, like the spouse limited access trust. Special needs trusts are ideal for someone who has children or family members with disabilities to be taken care of, and it makes sure their government benefits stay intact. A life insurance trust is ideal if you have a sizeable life insurance policy and don't want your estate to pay a lot in taxes when it is cashed out. Finally, the dynasty/legacy trust allows you to pass wealth down through the generations without it being taxed. Each one of these trusts has its advantages as well as disadvantages. Take time to research, consult a licensed attorney, and see which one is the most ideal for your family.

Also note that these various special trusts fall into two categories: revocable or irrevocable trusts. A revocable trust lets you maintain control of your assets during your lifetime. However, an irrevocable trust cannot be changed once terms are established. There are benefits to each category, depending on what you need and desire when establishing a trust.

Generational wealth is one of the best and biggest gifts you can provide for your children, grandchildren, and future heirs to your assets. Trusts will allow you to protect your assets and provide for your family after your demise. This is a beautiful way to create and establish a legacy that will be long-standing and far-reaching.

Concluding Remarks

Prosperity is within reach, but it requires a complete shift in thinking, knowledge, and continued effort. There is no get-rich-quick scheme that will lead you to prosperity, nor is there some financial "diet" you can go on to achieve the life you want—a lifestyle change must be enacted every single day. However, this book aims to give you a solid base to build upon, so keep learning and executing.

The goal is financial freedom. The path will be to read books, research a lot, evaluate your finances and objectives, and invest your time, money, and skills. The results are wealth creation and a legacy to leave to future generations. To achieve wealth and success, you must not be afraid to take risks with your money and with yourself. The tools, tips, and advice I have given you are the blueprint to financial freedom, but ultimately, you must decide that this is the road you want to drive down. This road may have obstacles that pop up, and you will have to go on a detour, but don't stop and turn around to go back to where you came from. You will have to sacrifice some things in the short term to achieve your long-term desires and goals.

Nevertheless, you want to leave a powerful legacy for your future generations so that they can continue on this road to greatness. Our ancestors had to endure struggles financially, mentally, and spiritually for us to be able to ride down this road. So don't be afraid to step out on faith and take some incredible risks so that you can gain some great rewards—our future generations depend on it. And remember, you don't want to die poor.

Bibliography

"A Beneficiary's Guide to Dynasty Trusts." n.d. Trust & Will. Accessed January 20, 2023. https://trustandwill.com/learn/dynasty-trusts-for-beneficiaries.

"Articles and Videos." n.d. Banking Truths. Accessed January 20, 2023. https://bankingtruths.com/articles-and-videos/.

Corley, Thomas C. 2009. *Rich Habits: The Daily Success Habits of Wealthy Individuals: Find out How the Rich Get so Rich (the Secrets to Financial Success Revealed)*. Minneapolis, Mn: Langdon Street Press.

"Free Estate Planning Information for Families and Individuals." n.d. The American College of Trust and Estate Counsel. Accessed January 20, 2023. https://www.actec.org/estate-planning/resources-for-families/.

"How a Bypass Trust Works in an Estate Plan." 2020. SmartAsset. March 19, 2020. https://smartasset.com/estate-planning/bypass-trust.

"How Cash Value Builds in a Life Insurance Policy." n.d. Investopedia. https://www.investopedia.com/articles/personal-finance/082114/how-cash-value-builds-life-insurance-policy.asp.

"IconTrust | Nevada Trust Company | Trustee Services." 2020. IconTrust | Nevada Trust Company | Trustee Services. October 22, 2020. https://icontrustnv.com/.

"Life Insurance Trusts." n.d. Www.nolo.com. Accessed January 20, 2023. https://www.nolo.com/legal-encyclopedia/life-insurance-trusts.html.

Michel, Kevin L. 2013. *Moving through Parallel Worlds to Achieve Your Dreams: The Epic Guide to Unlimited Power*. Kevin L. Michel.

"What Is a Marital Trust? How Does It Work? – Forbes Advisor." n.d. Www.forbes.com. Accessed January 20, 2023. https://www.forbes.com/advisor/investing/financial-advisor/marital-trust/.

"What Is Estate Planning? Estate Planning Basics." n.d. Trust & Will. https://trustandwill.com/learn/what-is-estate-planning.

Acknowledgments

First of all, I want to thank God for the countless blessings. Also, a big thanks to my entire family, who have continued to push me to write this book. Next, I want to thank my sister, Anita, for those initial edits; my friend, Damu, for being my accountability partner in completing this book; my public relations team for helping to get my brand out in the world; to all the people who help to educate me on financial literacy, and North Carolina A&T and Duke University for giving a poor kid from the South a quality education. Finally, I want to thank everyone who purchased a book or supported my various businesses.

About the Author

Rico is all about helping people achieve prosperity. He is an introvert, coach, philanthropist, investor, tech executive, entrepreneur, and father.

In his coaching practice, he shares the secrets to succeeding in your career, teaches financial literacy, how to create multiple income streams, and strategies to make your money work through investing.

In his career as a director of mergers & acquisitions for Intel Corporation, Rico is responsible for the financial valuation and acquisition of multimillion-dollar technology companies. Before working at Intel, Rico worked in various leadership roles at Verizon and Walmart Headquarters in strategy, finance, marketing, and supply chain.

Rico is also an entrepreneur and creator. He is the resourceful owner of *Snack 'n Fun Box*, a snack and activity box for kids. He is also the creator of *Color Me Back to the '90s* and *Sweet Pets* coloring books for adults and children. What's more, he is also an avid investor in stocks and real estate. Additionally, he is a certified coach for small business owners and professionals.

Rico is very involved in his community. For example, he created an endowment for business and entrepreneurship at North Carolina A&T State University to provide scholarships for students with business and economic degrees and budding entrepreneurs.

Rico is also an Air Force Veteran who served as a captain while on active duty. Additionally, he was responsible for tactical and satellite communication systems while deployed to Afghanistan during Operation Enduring Freedom. His decorations include an Air Force

Commendation Medal, Defense Service Medal, Humanitarian Service Medal, Afghanistan Campaign Medal, and Air Force Achievement Medal.

Rico is a North Carolina Agricultural and Technical State University graduate with a B.S. in Agriculture and Applied Economics. In addition, he has an M.B.A. from Duke University—The Fuqua School of Business—and an M.S. in Supply Chain Management from Georgia College. He is also a Certified Supply Chain Professional from APICS, the Association for Operations Management. He is a member of Kappa Alpha Psi Fraternity, having been initiated at the North Carolina A&T Chapter, the Alpha Nu Chapter.

Hi! I'm the real Rico. It's super weird to talk about myself in the third person. Real talk: even though I play an inspiring entrepreneur, coach, and author on the internet, I'm also a real person, an Air Force veteran, and a cancer survivor who grew up poor in the south to a single mother of four. As a troubled youth, I repeated the first grade and got into all kinds of trouble. Through hard work and faith, I eventually received three degrees and became a finance executive in Silicon Valley.

I'm passionate about changing the world. And one extremely impactful way to do that is to help people—especially women, veterans, and minorities—make more money and create a prosperous life. So, my role in the world is to help people earn more money so they can create prosperity for the people they love.

Follow me on Instagram and Facebook at @ricobeanscoaching!

Appendix A

20 Finance Terms Everyone Should Know

1. Amortization: Amortization is a method of spreading an intangible asset's cost over the course of its useful life. Intangible assets are nonphysical assets that are essential to a company, such as a trademark, patent, copyright, or franchise agreement.

2. Assets: Assets are items you own that can provide future benefit to your business, such as cash, inventory, real estate, office equipment, or accounts receivable, which are payments due to a company by its customers. There are different types of assets, including:

- Current Assets: These can be converted to cash within a year.
- Fixed Assets: These can't immediately be turned into cash but are tangible items that a company owns and uses to generate long-term income.

3. Asset Allocation: Asset allocation refers to how you choose to spread your money across different investment types, also known as asset classes. These include:

- Bonds: Bonds represent a form of borrowing. When you buy a bond, typically from the government or a corporation, you're essentially lending them money. You receive periodic interest payments and get back the loaned amount at the time of the bond's maturity—or the defined term at which the bond can be redeemed.
- Stocks: A stock is a share of ownership in a public or private company. When you buy stock in a company, you become a shareholder and can receive dividends—the company's profits—if and when they are distributed.
- Cash and Cash Equivalents: This refers to any asset in the form of cash or which can be converted to cash easily in the event it's necessary.

4. Balance Sheet: A balance sheet is an important financial statement communicating an organization's worth or "book value." The balance sheet includes a tally of the organization's assets, liabilities, and shareholders' equity for a given reporting period.

- The Balance Sheet Equation: Balance sheets are arranged according to the following equation: Assets = Liabilities + Owners' Equity.

5. Capital Gain: A capital gain is an increase in the value of an asset or investment above the price you initially paid for it. If you sell the asset for less than the original purchase price, that would be considered a capital loss.

6. Capital Market: This is a market where buyers and sellers engage in the trade of financial assets, including stocks and bonds. Capital markets feature several participants, including:

- Companies: Firms that sell stocks and bonds to investors.
- Institutional Investors: Investors who purchase stocks and bonds on behalf of a large capital base.
- Mutual Funds: A mutual fund is an institutional investor that manages the investments of thousands of individuals.
- Hedge Funds: A hedge fund is another type of institutional investor which controls risk through hedging—a process of buying one stock and then shorting a similar stock to make money from the difference in their relative performance.

7. Cash Flow: Cash flow refers to the net balance of cash moving in and out of a business at a specific point in time. Cash flow is commonly broken into three categories, including:

- Operating Cash Flow: The net cash generated from normal business operations.

- Investing Cash Flow: The net cash generated from investing activities, such as securities investments and the purchase or sale of assets.
- Financing Cash Flow: The net cash generated from financing a business, including debt payments, shareholders' equity, and dividend payments.

8. Cash Flow Statement: A cash flow statement is a financial statement prepared to provide a detailed analysis of what happened to a company's cash during a given period of time. This document shows how the business generated and spent its cash by including an overview of cash flows from operating, investing, and financing activities during the reporting period.

9. Compound Interest: This refers to "interest on interest." Rather, when you're investing or saving, compound interest is earned on the amount you deposited plus any interest you've accumulated over time. While it can grow your savings, it can also increase your debt; compound interest is charged on the initial amount you were loaned, as well as the expenses added to your outstanding balance over time.

10. Depreciation: Depreciation represents the decrease in an asset's value. It's a term commonly used in accounting and shows how much of an asset's value a business has used over a period of time.

11. EBITDA: An acronym standing for *EARNINGS BEFORE INTEREST, TAXES, DEPRECIATION, AND AMORTIZATION.* EBITDA is a commonly used measure of a company's ability to generate cash flow. To get EBITDA, you would add net profit, interest, taxes, depreciation, and amortization together.

12. Equity: Equity, often called shareholders' equity or owners' equity on a balance sheet, represents the amount of money that belongs to the owners of a business after all assets and liabilities have been accounted for. Using the accounting equation, shareholders' equity can be found by subtracting total liabilities from total assets.

13. Income Statement: An income statement is a financial statement that summarizes a business's income and expenses during a given period of time. An income statement is also sometimes referred to as a profit and loss (P&L) statement.

14. Liabilities: The opposite of assets, liabilities are what you owe other parties, such as bank debt, wages, and money due to suppliers, also known as accounts payable. There are different types of liabilities, including:

- Current Liabilities: Also known as short-term liabilities, these are what's due in the next year.
- Long-Term Liabilities: These are financial obligations not due over a year that can be paid off over a longer period of time.

15. Liquidity: Liquidity describes how quickly your assets can be converted into cash. Because of that, cash is the most liquid asset. The least liquid assets are items like real estate or land because they can take weeks or months to sell.

16. Net Worth: You can calculate net worth by subtracting what you own, your assets, from what you owe, your liabilities. The remaining number can help you determine the overall state of your financial health.

17. Profit Margin: Profit margin is a measure of profitability that's calculated by dividing the net income by revenue or the net profit by sales. Companies often analyze two types of profit margins:

- Gross Profit Margin: This typically applies to a specific product or line item rather than an entire business.
- Net Profit Margin: This typically represents the profitability of an entire company.

18. Return on Investment (ROI): Return on investment is a simple calculation used to determine the expected return of a project or activity in comparison to the cost of the investment, typically shown as a percentage. This measure is often used to evaluate whether a project will be worthwhile for a business to pursue. ROI is calculated by using the following equation: ROI = [(Income - Cost) / Cost] * 100.

19. Valuation: Valuation is the process of determining the current worth of an asset, company, or liability. There are a variety of ways you can value a business. But regularly repeating the process is helpful because you're then ready if ever faced with an opportunity to merge or sell your company or are trying to seek funding from outside investors.

20. Working Capital: Also known as net working capital, this is the difference between a company's current assets and current liabilities. Working capital—the money available for daily operations—can help determine an organization's operational efficiency and short-term financial health.

Appendix B

Investor Knowledge Quiz

How much do you really know about investing? Take this short quiz and test your knowledge. Answers follow after the quiz.

1. If you buy a company's stock . . .

a) You own a part of the company
b) You have lent money to the company
c) You are liable for the company's debts
d) The company will return your original investment to you with interest
e) Don't know/Not sure

2. If you buy a company's bond . . .

a) You own a part of the company
b) You have lent money to the company
c) You are liable for the company's debts
d) You can vote on shareholder resolutions
e) Don't know/Not sure

3. Which type of bond is the safest?

a) U.S. Treasury bond
b) Municipal bond
c) Corporate bond
d) Don't know/Not sure

4. In general, if interest rates go down, then bond prices . . .

a) Go down
b) Go up
c) Are not affected
d) Don't know/Not sure

5. Which of the following is the best definition for a "junk bond?"

a) A bond that is rated as "below investment grade" by rating agencies
b) A bond that has declined dramatically in value
c) A bond that has defaulted
d) A bond that is not regulated
e) Don't know/Not sure

6. A "no-load" mutual fund is one that . . .

a) Carries no fees
b) Carries no sales charge
c) Does not contain high-risk securities
d) Has no limits on the period of time in which it can be bought or sold
e) Don't know/Not sure

7. In general, investments that are riskier tend to provide higher returns over time than investments with less risk.

a) True
b) False
c) Don't know/Not sure

8. What is a reasonable average annual return that can be expected from a broadly diversified U.S. stock mutual fund over the long run?

a) 5%
b) 10%
c) 15%
d) 20%
e) 25%
f) Don't know/Not sure

9. Over the last 20 years in the U.S., the best average returns have been generated by:

a) Stocks
b) Bonds
c) CDs

d) Money market accounts
e) Precious metals
f) Don't know/Not sure

10. Which of the following organizations insures you against your losses in the stock market?

a) FDIC (Federal Deposit Insurance Corporation)
b) FINRA (Financial Industry Regulatory Authority)
c) SEC (Securities and Exchange Commission)
d) SIPC (Securities Investor Protection Corporation)
e) None of the above
f) Don't know/Not sure

11. If a company files for bankruptcy, which of the following securities are most at risk of becoming virtually worthless?

a) The company's preferred stock
b) The company's common stock
c) The company's bonds
d) Don't know/Not sure

12. Which of the following best explains why many municipal bonds pay lower yields than other government bonds?

a) Municipal bonds are lower risk
b) There is a greater demand for municipal bonds
c) Municipal bonds can be tax-free
d) Don't know/Not sure

13. You invest $500 to buy $1,000 worth of stock on margin. The value of the stock drops by 50 percent. You sell it. Approximately how much of your original $500 investment are you left within the end?

a) $500
b) $250
c) $0
d) Don't know/Not sure

14. Which is the best definition of "selling short?"

a) Selling shares of stock shortly after buying it
b) Selling shares of a stock before it has reached its peak
c) Selling shares of a stock at a loss
d) Selling borrowed shares of a stock
e) Don't know/Not sure

15. If you receive a margin call that gives you 15 days to deposit additional cash or securities in your account, your broker cannot sell any of the securities in your account until after 15 days.

a) True
b) False
c) Don't know/Not sure

16. Hedge funds are always subject to the same rules and regulations as mutual funds.

a) True
b) False
c) Don't know/Not sure

17. The principal difference between mutual fund share classes (Class A, Class B, Class C, etc.) are:

a) The different investments each class makes
b) The different fees and expenses each class charges
c) The different investment advisers in charge of managing each class
d) Don't know/Not sure

18. A Section 529 Plan is a tax-advantaged way to save for:

a) College
b) Retirement
c) Long-term health care
d) Don't know/Not sure

Answers

1. If you buy a company's stock . . .

a) You own a part of the company
b) You have lent money to the company
c) You are liable for the company's debts
d) The company will return your original investment to you with interest
e) Don't know/Not sure

The correct answer is (a).

Stocks are known as "equities" because each stock share represents a small percentage of ownership in the company, entitling the shareholder to vote in the election of directors and on other matters taken up at the shareholder meetings or by proxy.

2. If you buy a company's bond . . .

a) You own a part of the company
b) You have lent money to the company
c) You are liable for the company's debts
d) You can vote on shareholder resolutions
e) Don't know/Not sure

The correct answer is (b).

Bonds are loans that investors make to a corporation or a government body in exchange for regular interest payments and the return of principal at a future date. Companies issue corporate bonds to raise money for capital expenditures, operations, and acquisitions. But unlike stockholders, bondholders don't receive ownership rights in the corporation.

3. Which type of bond is the safest?

a) U.S. Treasury bond
b) Municipal bond
c) Corporate bond
d) Don't know/Not sure

The correct answer is (a).

"Treasuries" are issued by the federal government. Unlike corporate or municipal bonds, they are backed by the "full faith and credit" of the U.S. government, which guarantees that interest payments will always be made, and the bonds redeemed at maturity.

4. In general, if interest rates go down, then bond prices . . .

a) Go down
b) Go up
c) Are not affected
d) Don't know/Not sure

The correct answer is (b).

The cardinal rule of bonds: When interest rates fall, bond prices rise, and when interest rates rise, bond prices fall. This is because as interest rates go up, newer bonds come to market paying higher interest yields than older bonds already in the hands of investors, making the older bonds worth less.

5. Which of the following is the best definition for a "junk bond?"

a) A bond that is rated as "below investment grade" by rating agencies
b) A bond that has declined dramatically in value
c) A bond that has defaulted
d) A bond that is not regulated
e) Don't know/Not sure

The correct answer is (a).

"Junk" or "high-yield" bonds are issued by companies with poor credit ratings, meaning that compared with better-rated "investment-grade" bonds, the risk is greater that these companies will default on their interest payments or even go bankrupt and be unable to redeem their bonds when they mature. To attract investors, "junk" bonds pay higher yields than higher-graded corporate bonds.

6. A "no-load" mutual fund is one that . . .

a) Carries no fees
b) Carries no sales charge
c) Does not contain high-risk securities
d) Has no limits on the period of time in which it can be bought or sold
e) Don't know/Not sure

The correct answer is (b).

Not all mutual funds charge sales loads. Called no-load funds, these funds do not charge a front-end sales charge or a deferred sales charge, such as a Contingent Deferred Sales Charge (CDSC). In addition, the fund's 12b-1 fees must not exceed 0.25 percent of the fund's average annual net assets in order to call itself a no-load fund. No-load funds can be purchased directly from a mutual fund company or brokerage firm fund supermarket, but you won't receive the assistance of a broker or investment professional. For those wanting professional advice, no-load funds also may be purchased through an investment adviser or broker, but you'll typically pay a fee for this advice. This means you will be paying a fee on top of the underlying mutual fund expenses.

7. In general, investments that are riskier tend to provide higher returns over time than investments with less risk.

a) True
b) False
c) Don't know/Not sure

The correct answer is (a).

The stock and bond markets tend to reward risk-taking over the long term. This is called the risk-reward tradeoff. Over the short term, however, high-risk investments such as small-company stocks can be extremely volatile. The less willing you are to take that risk, the more you may want to emphasize investments that provide a regular return with less volatility, such as short-term bonds.

8. What is a reasonable average annual return that can be expected from a broadly diversified U.S. stock mutual fund over the long run?

a) 5%
b) 10%
c) 15%
d) 20%
e) 25%
f) Don't know/Not sure

The correct answer is (b).

Over a long period— such as 20 years or more—the U.S. stock market has historically returned average annualized returns of about 10 percent. However, over a shorter period, the stock market may experience a severe decline in value, including for several years at a time during a "bear" market.

9. Over the last 20 years in the U.S., the best average returns have been generated by:

a) Stocks
b) Bonds
c) CDs
d) Money market accounts
e) Precious metals
f) Don't know/Not sure

The correct answer is (a).

The average annualized returns for the U.S. stock market over the last 20 years have outpaced the return on bonds or other "safer" investments. The stock market has historically been the best-performing long-term investment vehicle, although equities can be extremely volatile, and the stock market will experience sharp declines over a period of several years at a time.

10. Which of the following organizations insures you against your losses in the stock market?

a) FDIC (Federal Deposit Insurance Corporation)
b) FINRA (Financial Industry Regulatory Authority)
c) SEC (Securities and Exchange Commission)
d) SIPC (Securities Investor Protection Corporation)
e) None of the above
f) Don't know/Not sure

The correct answer is (e).

When you invest in stocks, you accept the risk that your investment may decline as well as rise in value. A primary role of securities regulators such as FINRA and the SEC is to ensure that securities laws and regulations are followed and to punish violators. The FDIC generally insures checking, savings, and other deposit accounts when an FDIC-regulated bank fails.

The mission of the Securities Investor Protection Corporation (SIPC) is to return funds and securities to investors if the brokerage firm holding these assets becomes insolvent.

11. If a company files for bankruptcy, which of the following securities are most at risk of becoming virtually worthless?

a) The company's preferred stock
b) The company's common stock
c) The company's bonds
d) Don't know/Not sure

The correct answer is (b).

Among those with claims to a bankrupt company's assets, shareholders of common stock have the last claim on any assets, falling in line behind secured creditors, bondholders, and owners of preferred shares. Common shareholders may not receive anything if the secured and unsecured creditors' claims are not fully repaid.

12. Which of the following best explains why many municipal bonds pay lower yields than other government bonds?

a) Municipal bonds are lower risk
b) There is a greater demand for municipal bonds
c) Municipal bonds can be tax-free
d) Don't know/Not sure

The correct answer is (c).

Because dividend payments from municipal bonds are usually exempt from federal income tax, even with lower yields than other government bonds, their after-tax rates of return are attractive to investors in higher tax brackets.

13. You invest $500 to buy $1,000 worth of stock on margin. The value of the stock drops by 50 percent. You sell it. Approximately how much of your original $500 investment are you left within the end?

a) $500
b) $250
c) $0
d) Don't know/Not sure

The correct answer is (c).

When you buy stock on margin, you risk losing your entire investment—or much more. In this example, an investor used $500 to buy $1,000 worth of stock, borrowing the additional $500 from a brokerage firm to make the purchase. When the stock was sold after dropping 50 percent in value, its remaining worth was only $500—

the same amount the investor still owed to the brokerage firm for the margin loan.

14. Which is the best definition of "selling short?"

a) Selling shares of stock shortly after buying it
b) Selling shares of a stock before it has reached its peak
c) Selling shares of a stock at a loss
d) Selling borrowed shares of a stock
e) Don't know/Not sure

The correct answer is (d).

Short selling involves borrowing stock from a broker through a margin account and selling it, with the understanding that it must later be bought back and returned to the broker.

If the stock declines in value, as the short seller hopes, the investor will profit since the value of the stock borrowed and sold would be higher than the stock subsequently purchased and returned to the broker. However, if the stock rises in value, the investor must pay the difference to make good on the stock owed to the broker.

NASD Rule 3350, the Short Sale Rule, sets forth restrictions for short sales of NASDAQ National Market® securities.*

15. If you receive a margin call that gives you 15 days to deposit additional cash or securities in your account, your broker cannot sell any of the securities in your account until after 15 days.

a) True
b) False
c) Don't know/Not sure

The correct answer is (b).

Some investors mistakenly believe that a firm must contact them first for a margin call to be valid. This is not the case. Most firms will attempt to notify their customers of margin calls, but they are not required to do so. Even if you're contacted and provided with a specific date to meet a margin call, your firm may decide to sell some or all of your securities before that date without any further notice to you. For example, your firm may take this action because the market value of your securities has continued to decline in value.

16. Hedge funds are always subject to the same rules and regulations as mutual funds.

a) True
b) False
c) Don't know/Not sure

The correct answer is (b).

Hedge funds are basically private investment pools. Because they are usually only open to limited numbers of wealthy, financially sophisticated investors and do not advertise or publicly offer their securities, private hedge funds are usually not required to register with the SEC. As a result, unregistered private hedge funds do not provide many of the investor protections that apply to registered investment products, such as mutual funds. For example, hedge funds generally are not subject to numerous mutual fund rules, such as regulations requiring a certain degree of liquidity, limiting how much can be invested in any one investment, and protecting against conflicts of interest.

17. The principal difference between mutual fund share classes (Class A, Class B, Class C, etc.) are:

a) The different investments each class makes
b) The different fees and expenses each class charges
c) The different investment advisers in charge of managing each class
d) Don't know/Not sure

The correct answer is (b).

A single mutual fund, with one portfolio and one investment adviser, may offer more than one "class" of its shares to investors. Each class represents a similar interest in the mutual fund's portfolio. The principal difference between the classes is that the mutual fund will charge you different fees and expenses depending on the class that you choose. If you are thinking about choosing a mutual fund with more than one class, it is important for you to understand the differences between them.

18. A Section 529 Plan is a tax-advantaged way to save for:

a) College
b) Retirement
c) Long-term health care
d) Don't know/Not sure

The correct answer is (a). Named after the section of the federal tax code that governs them; Section 529 plans are tax-advantaged programs that help families save for college.

Appendix C

Smart Goals Sheet

SMART

GOALS

WHEN SETTING GOALS, MAKE SURE IT FOLLOWS THE SMART STRUCTURE.
USE THE QUESTIONS BELOW TO CREATE YOUR GOALS.

S	SPECIFIC WHAT DO I WANT TO ACCOMPLISH?	
M	MEASURABLE HOW WILL I KNOW WHEN IT IS ACCOMPLISHED?	
A	ACHIEVABLE HOW CAN THE GOAL BE ACCOMPLISHED?	
R	RELEVANT DOES THIS SEEM WORTHWHILE?	
T	TIME BOUND WHEN CAN I ACCOMPLISH THIS GOAL?	

Appendix D

Income & Expense Tracker

INCOME + EXPENSE TRACKER

YEAR: _______________

MONTH	INCOME	EXPENSES	BALANCE
January			
February			
March			
April			
June			
July			
August			
September			
October			
November			
December			
TOTAL			

RICO BEANS COACHING

Appendix E

Savings Tracker

SAVINGS TRACKER

YEAR OF	SAVING FOR	AMOUNT NEEDED

MONTH	WEEK 1	WEEK 2	WEEK 3	WEEK 4	TOTAL
JANUARY					
FEBRUARY					
MARCH					
APRIL					
MAY					
JUNE					
JULY					
AUGUST					
SEPTEMBER					
OCTOBER					
NOVEMBER					
DECEMBER					

RICO BEANS COACHING

Printed in Poland
by Amazon Fulfillment
Poland Sp. z o.o., Wrocław

32129200R00090